Slavery and Servitude in
Colonial North America
A Short History

KENNETH MORGAN

NEW YORK UNIVERSITY PRESS
Washington Square, New York

First published in the U.S.A. in 2001 by
NEW YORK UNIVERSITY PRESS
Washington Square
New York, NY 10003

First published in the UK by
Edinburgh University Press Ltd
22 George Square, Edinburgh

Typeset in Monotype Fournier
by Bibliocraft, Dundee, and
printed and bound in Great Britain
by MPG Books Ltd, Bodmin

CIP data available from the Library of Congress
ISBN 0-8147-5669-7 (cloth)
ISBN 0-8147-5670-0 (pbk.)

Contents

Introduction

This book concentrates on an important sub-field of early American history that is crucial for understanding not just colonial North America but the later development of the United States. During the seventeenth and eighteenth centuries, North America was predominantly an agricultural, pre-industrial society and economy in which the factors of production were unevenly distributed. Capital was scarce in the North American colonies until British traders and settlers undertook the pioneering tasks of investing in the land and resources there. Though land was always abundant in North America, in the seventeenth century it was not always freely available. Indian settlements over certain territories, proprietorial rights granted by royal decree, and private joint-stock company claims made access to land problematic. In addition, labour was always needed to make natural resources productive. For North America in the early modern era, such labour consisted of either a stream of British and European white immigrants or the importation of enslaved Africans. Free wage labour was always scarce in the American colonies, either because it was too expensive or too undependable. Thus the chief characteristic of labour in British America became compulsory work for specified terms of years or for life. Three-quarters of the immigrants who peopled the American colonies experienced unfree labour for at least part of their lives. Servants constituted between a half and two-thirds of these migrants and, together with slaves, comprised the majority of the working population in the thirteen mainland colonies under British rule.

Slavery and servitude have attracted much innovative and imaginative scholarship over the past three decades. One important stimulus has been the rise of social history as a prominent feature of historical writing, with attention paid to mining a rich quarry of qualitative and quantitative sources, using appropriate methodologies to match, and a concern to understand the ordinary lives of the people who made America. Another stimulus has been the revival of interest in Atlantic history, whereby historians trace the demographic, economic, cultural and geographical features of life in the transition from the Old World to the New, placing the experiences of immigrants in a broad context of time and place. Much of this writing, however, is scattered in monographs, articles and contributions to symposia; there is no up-to-date textbook on slavery in colonial North America, let alone one dealing with slavery and servitude. This book offers, I hope, a helpful overview and a timely synthesis of the most prominent labour institutions in early North America.

The time-scale covered by the book comprises the two centuries from 1600 to 1800. Permanent English settlement in North America only began in 1607 with the founding of Jamestown, under the auspices of the Virginia Company, in the Chesapeake tidewater. Though free white migrants were the first group of settlers to till the land there, the colony of Virginia soon attracted indentured servants as the majority of its workers, and so this period in the early seventeenth century is an appropriate starting point for the book. It might be thought that 1776 would be a logical closing date for the analysis: American independence and the establishment of a republic were the crucial political and constitutional turning points in the creation of the American nation. However, 1776 is not so helpful an end point for examining the development of labour institutions such as servitude and slavery. By opting for 1800 as an approximate closing date for the book, one can show the impact of the American Revolution on slaves and, to a lesser extent, servants. By taking the story through the era of the Federal Constitution and the first years of national government one can analyze the degree to which notions of liberty, equality and freedom – central tenets of the founding of the United States – impacted on attitudes towards slavery, abolitionism and the growth of free labour. By concluding around 1800 one can also trace the decline of indentured servitude to the point where it was insignificant in North America, and cut off the discussion of slavery before the antebellum period – on which there are a plethora of studies.

The book is organized thematically, with attention paid to changes in servitude and slavery over time and in place. In common with the regional focus of the current historiography on early North America, four main regions are referred to repeatedly throughout the book. These are New England, the Middle Colonies/states, the Chesapeake (or Upper South) and the Lower South. Enslaved Africans and servants lived in all four regions. They were, however, disproportionately located in the two southern regions, where plantations were the most prominent form of agricultural cultivation, and so the discussion in this study reflects the importance of Virginia, Maryland, the Carolinas and Georgia to the evolution of slave and servant labour in early North America. Some chapters combine aspects of slavery and servitude; others treat these topics separately. Throughout the entire book some overriding themes reappear, almost as *leitmotifs*: the geographic background of the unfree labour force; the work routines of white and black bound labourers and their contribution to different regional economies; the significance of racial attitudes and distinctions; supply and demand factors in transatlantic migration and labour; and resistance to bondage. Though occasional references are made to slavery and servitude in the British Caribbean colonies, the focus throughout this volume is on the North American mainland, in keeping with the aims of the series in which it appears.

The book opens with a detailed chapter examining indentured servitude in seventeenth-century North America. The reasons why such migrants outnumbered free white emigrants in several American regions provide a framework for the chapter, along with English settlers' initial preference for a white labour force. The discussion looks at the social and economic background of servants in England, their geographic mobility, and their links to the 'servants in husbandry' that were a notable feature of the labouring poor in early modern England. Attention is given to the debate over the background status of these migrants: whether they were 'middling people' or a representative cross-section of the working population of seventeenth-century England. As well as supply conditions, the demand for servants is examined in relation to prices, labour opportunities, the paucity of free wage labour in early North America, and fluctuations over time. The distribution of servants is discussed, especially for the Chesapeake, their main destination across the Atlantic in this period. The chapter concludes with an assessment of the opportunities (or lack thereof) for ex-servants seeping into the free white population at the end of their service.

The focus of Chapter 2 is the transition from servitude to slavery in the period c. 1670 to 1720, with particular reference to the staple plantation colonies: Virginia, Maryland and the Carolinas. The relative decline of indentured servitude in these areas is related to supply problems and demographic change in England and to white Virginians' fears about being overrun by landless ex-servants during a period of social turbulence in the 1670s and 1680s. The chapter shows that the choice of slaves as a substitute labour force was by no means automatic. This entails discussion of why Native Americans were not enslaved by whites to a large extent (even though they themselves, in some instances, were slaveowners). The beginnings of large-scale English slave trading after the Restoration are outlined. Three issues about the widespread adoption of slave labour on plantations are analyzed in depth: first, whether racial prejudice preceded slavery or whether it occurred largely after slaves became plantation labourers; second, whether slaves were preferred to servants mainly for economic reasons; and third, why the timing of the transition from a servant to a slave labour force differed in the Chesapeake and the Carolinas.

Chapter 3 analyzes the changing nature of servitude in eighteenth-century North America, revealing how it became wider in its composition and regional background. Indentured servants were now Scotch-Irish and Irish as well English. Convicts from the British Isles became a significant segment of the servant population after the Transportation Act was passed in 1718. A new and sizeable servant group from the 1720s onwards consisted of German redemptioners. The supply conditions relating to these various groups are discussed, as well as the differing demand for them in North America: something related to their skills and the changing labour requirements of various regions. The similarities and differences of these groups are outlined. The criminality of convicts is also considered, both with regard to the offences they had been sentenced for in Britain and the perception of their propensity to crime in the Chesapeake. Part of the chapter focuses on the argument made for Pennsylvania servants – in the most extended study of eighteenth-century servitude – that minimal overt conflict between masters and servants in the late seventeenth century was replaced by harsher dealings with bonded servants thereafter, as witnessed in the emergence of written indentures rather than oral contracts, longer terms of service, and harsher, more exploitative master–servant relations.

Chapter 4 traces the evolution of slavery in mainland North America during the eighteenth century. This potentially vast subject is made manageable by concentration on certain major themes. The regional dimension of slavery underpins the analysis, so that the role of slaves in New England, the Middle Colonies, the Chesapeake and the Lower South can be delineated. The economic base of slavery and the skilled and unskilled labour performed by slaves, both on and off plantations, in urban and rural settings, is considered. Attention focuses here on the use of the gang and task systems in different locales. The different regional demography of slavery is examined, along with its implications for family life. The living arrangements of slaves are also covered, with reference to the innovative work carried out by archaeologists. Master–slave relations form an important part of the discussion. The sorts of questions answered here are as follows. To what extent did slaveowners regard themselves as patriarchs? Did they try to maintain paternalist relations over slaves under their control? What degree of autonomy did slaves achieve in their work and domestic lives? To what extent were African cultural practices preserved? Should one emphasize the achievements of blacks under slavery? Or rather, should emphasis fall on the manipulative control of white masters? How were slaves treated under the law?

Slaves and servants were often unhappy about their lot, and so Chapter 5 investigates the different types of resistance to unfree labour in early North America. These include day-to-day resistance such as work stoppages, running away, and rebellions. The composition and motives of slave, servant and convict runaways in different regions are delineated. The general lack of concerted rebellion or resistance by these groups and the difficulties they faced in acting together are explained. This is then related to racial prejudice and class links among these workers. There is also discussion of slave resistance during the revolutionary era. Three rebellions are considered in terms of their motives, organization and failure to succeed: Bacon's Rebellion in Virginia (1676), the Stono Rebellion in South Carolina (1739) and Gabriel's Rebellion in Virginia (1800).

The final chapter explores the themes of slavery and freedom in North America in the period from 1770 until 1800. Its main purpose is to explore the paradoxical coexistence of slavery and freedom in the revolutionary era. The treatment of slavery and the slave trade in some crucial documents of the revolutionary era is highlighted, with reference to the Declaration of Independence, the Articles of Confederation, the Northwest Ordinance, and the Federal Constitution of the United States. The attitudes of the Founding Fathers towards slavery are dissected, notably the views of the Virginian trio of George Washington, James Madison and Thomas Jefferson. Attempts to free slaves in the Northern and Middle states by gradual emancipation or manumission provisions are considered, and contrasted with the intransigence of the

Lower South in wishing to maintain slavery. These contrasting responses are related to the significance of slavery for the economies of different North American areas and the varying regional numbers of slaves. The growth of anti-slavery thought is analyzed and slavery explained as an aberration to human progress in the Enlightenment era. The role of blacks in the War of Independence and their embracing of Christianity as a moral force are also considered, so that the discussion is not merely about the actions of white men and women but about the activities of blacks as well.

In writing the book, I have drawn on many fine studies by other historians as well as summarizing some of my own research in this area. I hope I have not too liberally taken material from others without indicating the source of the information or ideas. Anyone who has attempted a broad synthesis will know that the word limit always seems tight. If in places my analyses lack some subtle nuances it is largely the result (I hope) of having to provide a succinct overview of a large, and sometimes contentious, area of early American history. A detailed bibliography, arranged by chapter, points up some of the most significant studies available. This will be useful particularly to students wanting to follow up my discussions by referring to more specialized works. Detailed footnoting seemed to me inappropriate in a textbook such as this one. Accordingly, I have only supplied endnotes to each chapter for direct quotations plus specific references to individual historians and their works mentioned in the text. For reasons of space, statistical tables are kept to a minimum but the text itself has a quantitative framework to indicate the broad parameters of slavery and servitude in North America before 1800.

As for nomenclature, there is the thorny problem of political correctness. A recent article on slavery that I submitted to an academic journal came back with a comment from one anonymous reviewer that I had over-used the word 'slave'. The critique argued that this obscured the fact that most slaves were transplanted Africans, and that one should call them 'Africans' in recognition of their humanity and not overplay the status given to them by others. Having duly revised the piece, another reviewer complained that I kept referring to 'Africans' in a discussion of slavery, the point being that this tended to ignore the fact that they were defined by their chattel status as slaves, and that 'slaves' was the appropriate word to use. Clearly, this is an aspect of writing about slavery that holds many hostages to fortune. Given that the fashionable or acceptable terminology has changed several times already during my adult lifetime, in this book I have used the terms 'African', 'slave', 'enslaved African' and 'black' interchangeably; and in doing so I hope I have not caused offence.

CHAPTER I

Indentured Servitude in the Seventeenth Century

This chapter mainly focuses on the Chesapeake because that was the destination for the majority of English indentured servants emigrating to North America in the seventeenth century. Of the 200,000 people who crossed the Atlantic from England to North America in that period, 120,000 (60 per cent) went either to Virginia, founded by the Virginia Company in 1607, or to Maryland, established by Lord Baltimore in 1634. The peak period for emigration was the three decades after 1630. Around three-quarters of the emigrants were indentured servants, so called because they signed a written contract or indenture before boarding ship to start a new life across the ocean. The indenture was a printed document with spaces left for details to be inserted of the name and age of the emigrant, the name of the ship captain, the witnesses, and, in some cases, the length of the contract. Usually indentured servants had their ship passage paid by the captain in return for the sale of their labour for periods of between three and seven years after they reached their destination. Servants arriving in the Chesapeake without written indentures had their time of service regulated according to the 'custom of the country'; in other words, they were subject to local laws and practices. Local courts dealt with such servants in order to determine their age and period of service. In seventeenth-century Virginia and Maryland, servants arriving without indentures usually served for four years if they were over 20, for between six and eight years if they were aged 16–20, and until the age of 21 if they were under 16 years old on arrival.

The servants, whether indentured or admitted according to the 'custom of the country', would then live in their new master's household, where they were given board and lodging but no wages or other compensation for their term of service. Their contracts could be transferred from one master to another without the servant's consent. While under indenture, servants were in a dependent position; they were single people who were not allowed to marry until they were independent. At the end of their term servants were usually entitled to freedom dues, which consisted of goods and sometimes land, so that they could become independent settlers. These dues varied from colony to colony, and over time, and were determined mainly by local customary practice, though some legislation also specified their exact nature. In Virginia land and clothing were given to newly-expired servants up to 1626 but thereafter no land was granted to servants at the end of their terms. A Virginian Act of 1705 stated that on completion of their term male servants could claim from their masters ten bushels of corn, thirty shillings or the equivalent, and a musket valued at a minimum of twenty shillings; female servants were entitled to fifteen bushels of corn and forty shillings in money or goods. A Maryland Act of 1640 specified the freedom dues in that province as 'one good Cloth suite of Keirsy or broad cloth a Shift of white linen one new pair of stockins and Shoes two hoes one axe 3 barrells of Corne and fifty acres of land ... women Servants a Years Provision of Corne and a like proportion of Cloths & Land.'[1] A later Maryland statute of 1663 made the allowance of land as part of freedom dues no longer obligatory. In 1698 it was reported in Maryland that servants, on completing their terms, 'are well lookt on, and theire masters cloathe them well and give them all other necessaryes for one year. And those that be Industrious and frugall purchase Estates, but negligent and careless persons run the Same fate here as in other Countryes.'[2]

Merchants shipping servants to the Chesapeake could claim a headright of fifty acres per person brought into Virginia. In Maryland the headright system operated differently, the fifty acres until 1683 being given to the time-expired servant and consisting of a warrant for land that was sufficient to pay for a survey plus a patent for a piece of land that had been located. The award of headrights was different from freedom dues: it is important not to confuse the two. Since freehold land lay beyond the means of most of the lower orders in seventeenth-century England, arrangements that included land rights in America might seem an attractive enticement for servants. But, as this summary has shown, the reality for servants was less rosy. Land given as part of freedom dues ended very early in the history of Virginia and had effectively been curtailed in Maryland by the early Restoration period. The headright system benefited shippers rather than servants in Virginia. In Maryland ex-servants needed capital from another source because the headright did not actually pay for the fifty acres of land.

The system of indenture was more formal than most existing labour arrangements obtaining in England during the early modern era; but it did not emerge in a vacuum. For generations, young Englishmen had been apprenticed to masters in trades, with the masters providing shelter and food for their charges, acting in *loco parentis*, and training the young person in a useful craft. Apprenticeship was a dependent position that usually lasted for seven years, commonly between the ages of fourteen and twenty-one. Most urban centres in Elizabethan and Stuart England had robust traditions of apprenticeship. In rural England there were other hiring arrangements for labour in which adolescents and young adults predominated. Verbal agreements for the year or for seasonal work were made, notably at hiring fairs, and agricultural work was commonly based around the labour of 'servants in husbandry'. Like indentured servants crossing the Atlantic, these were young, single, agricultural workers, who lived in their owners' dwellings, with free board and lodging, often with annual contracts. But they were not legal contracts; they tended to reflect customary practices. These servants were usually aged between fifteen and twenty-five and had not yet acquired an independent trade. In these respects the two labour institutions were similar, though certainly not identical. Some historians accordingly have seen indentured servitude as an extension of the position of servants in husbandry. The chief difference between the two lay in the more formal arrangements of the written indenture and the fact that servants in husbandry, unlike indentured servants, could not be bought or sold without their consent.

The characteristics of indentured emigrants and their reasons for migrating are explained below. Demand in the Chesapeake for indentured servants stemmed from the agricultural needs of settlers in a situation where free emigrants were in the minority, free wage labour was expensive, and population growth among the white population was problematic. Once tobacco was cultivated widely in the tidewater areas of the Chesapeake, from the mid-1620s onwards, a readily available cheap workforce was necessary to make profits. Before that time emigration to the Chesapeake was often temporary and generally unimportant, but servitude had already made its mark. In 1619 John Pory, secretary of Virginia, wrote that 'all our riches for the presente doe consiste in Tobacco', adding that 'our principal wealth consisteth in servants'.[3] An early Virginia census of 1624 listed 1,200 inhabitants in the colony (excluding Native Americans), 40 per cent of whom were servants. Thereafter the population of the Old Dominion, swelled by new emigrants, reached 7,600 in 1640, 12,000 in 1650 and 20,900 in 1660. Population levels were lower in Maryland: only 600 inhabitants lived there in 1640, rising to 4,000 in 1660. Africans could be found in the Chesapeake by the mid-seventeenth century, but at that time less than 5 per cent of the combined black and white population of the region consisted of blacks.

Indentured servants were more productive to engage – estimating their potential output by the price paid for them – than hired daily or weekly workers. They remained in high demand for most of the seventeenth century because of the skewed population among white settlers in Virginia and Maryland. This unbalanced sex ratio arose because most indentured labourers were young male adults: disproportionately so, for men outnumbered women by six to one among migrants to the Chesapeake in the 1630s. This fact, coupled with the extensive disease environment of the early Chesapeake, meant that family formation was slower than in areas with a better balance between the sexes. Gradually, this situation changed as the 'seasoning' problems of early Chesapeake settlers diminished; but it was not until the eighteenth century that a more balanced distribution of males and females existed among the white population in that region. In New England, where family migrations from the Old World plus a rise in fertility had led to rapid demographic growth, a more balanced sex ratio was the norm even in the first half of the seventeenth century. Servants, usually without indentures, constituted about one-third of the initial workforce of New England, but few were imported after the Great Migration of the 1630s. Family labour in large households became the norm. As an anonymous writer put it in the middle of the seventeenth century, 'Virginia thrives by keeping many servants, and these in strict obedience. New England conceive they and their Children can doe enough, and soe have rarely above one Servant.'[4]

Characteristics of Indentured Servants

The chief characteristics of indentured servants can be reconstructed from surviving lists of servant registrations. These only cover a minority of the servant flow overseas in the seventeenth century, but they are the best surviving sources for determining the age structure, occupational distribution, and geographic and social origins of this group of migrants. London was the largest English port of embarkation for indentured servants, but the principal registration list is one for Bristol covering the period 1654–86. This provides information on over 10,000 servants who sailed from the 'metropolis of the west' to the New World. Table 1.1 shows the colonial destinations to which these passengers travelled. Smaller registration lists are available for 390 servants leaving London for the Chesapeake between 1682 and 1686, for 483 servants listed in the Middlesex Quarter Sessions records in 1683 and 1684, and for 1,300 servants bound to Virginia and Maryland listed in Liverpool Corporation records for the decade after 1697. There are gaps in these sources but they are still the most useful data available for analyzing the servants' social characteristics: there are no equivalent records for free emigrants. The servant lists have been investigated microscopically by James Horn, David Galenson and David Souden in particular, and their findings can be summarized here.[5]

Far more male servants emigrated than females: the ratio was usually two-to-one or three-to-one. This reflected the need for productive, industrious field workers in the Chesapeake and the assumption that this was better provided by men than women. The unbalanced sex ratio among servants arriving in the Chesapeake – something also characteristic of free emigrants to that region in the seventeenth century – had important demographic and social implications that will be discussed

Table 1.1 Number of servant emigrants from Bristol to the New World, 1654–86

Year	Virginia	Maryland	New England	British Caribbean	Other Colonies	Total
1654–58*	542	0	7	1,022	479	2,050
1659–63	1,422	13	55	1,613	231	3,334
1664–68	1,117	8	25	471	21	1,642
1669–73	759	39	28	430	37	1,293
1674–78	880	42	34	371	32	1,360
1679–86**	154	35	13	486	27	715

* Entries for 1654 begin on 25 September.
** Figures for this period are incomplete.
Source: Abbot Emerson Smith, *Colonists in Bondage: White Servitude and Convict Labor in America, 1607–1776* (Chapel Hill: University of North Carolina Press, 1947), p. 309.

below. Most male and female servants covered by the lists were in the age range from fifteen to twenty-four. This tight age clustering suggests that few emigrated in family groups. The servants were overwhelmingly single, the majority of either sex being beneath the average (rather high) age of first marriage for men and women in seventeenth century England (which was twenty-eight and twenty-six years respectively). The age of first marriage in pre-industrial European societies reflected the age at which most people could expect to have the means to set up independent households, forge permanent partnerships, and afford families, children being more important for family incomes than in modern post-industrial society. Indentured servant migrants, by definition, lacked the capital characterized by this stage of the life cycle. Their decision to emigrate meant they were willing to delay entry into wedlock until they had completed their service and achieved independence in America. Most of those who married there did so fairly soon, it seems, after their contract had finished. Whether indentured servants had sufficient calculation or intelligence to realize that emigration to America, despite the obstacles, would usually enable them to marry earlier than at home is unknown.

Very little information is recorded on female occupations. There is considerably more data, however, for the males. In the Bristol list covering 1654–86, 44 per cent of the men with stated occupations referred to themselves as yeomen (or small freeholders). These were followed by semi-skilled and unskilled men, mainly labourers, comprising 21 per cent of the occupations. The other significant group, accounting for 14.5 per cent of the occupations, was workers in the textile and clothing trades. Altogether sixty-six different trades were represented in the Bristol list. Thirty-four trades were given in the list of London servants emigrating in 1683–4. Two conclusions that can be drawn from these statistics are that white servants included men from a wide variety of trades, and that the predominance of yeomen sailing from Bristol underscores the significance of the middling orders among the emigrants. Determining the social status of the servants before they sailed overseas is nevertheless complicated by the fact that most individuals listed had no stated occupation. Whether one regards this as an omission of skills and trades that they actually possessed or as a signal that they were unskilled will influence any conclusions about their social status. This technical matter has attracted considerable scholarly debate, and is analyzed in a separate section later in the chapter.

Most servants originated from the hinterlands of Bristol, Liverpool and London. Over 60 per cent of the servants in the Bristol list whose geographical origins are stated came from Bristol itself or from a forty-mile radius of the city. Between 1654 and 1660, for which data are almost complete, 35 per cent of indentured servants leaving Bristol came from within twenty miles of the city and 77 per cent from less than sixty miles. They were drawn from the market towns, villages and country-side of south Gloucestershire, north Somerset, and south Wales. But there was 'no clustering of servants from particular communities such as was found in the case of the Puritan migration' of the 1630s.[6] Sixty per cent of these migrants came from urban centres, whereas around 80 per cent of the English population as a whole were rural dwellers. A similar catchment area obtained for the servants in the Liverpool list: 70 per cent came from within a forty-mile radius of the port. The situation was different for servants leaving London in 1683–4: over half gave the metropolis as their origin, but the rest came from all over England. Horn argues that many of the latter had been born elsewhere, and that by putting down London they were specifying their current residence.[7] This could well be true, given the magnetic attraction of the metropolis for those undertaking internal migration, but it has not been proven.

Recruitment and Shipment

Potential emigrants willing to become indentured servants were recruited in and around major English ports with transatlantic shipping connections. In the seventeenth century, this meant London and Bristol for the most part, the leading two ports in the kingdom. In one sense, indentured servants selected themselves for emigration. As the previous section has shown, they came from the pool of migrants who had searched for work in various English settings at times of poor wages and unpromising economic opportunities at home. Generally young and single, they had often migrated internally more than once within England, usually over relatively short distances, in search of work. The geographical background of the servants on the Bristol list suggests that unemployment in urban trades was a particular stimulus to such mobility in the mid-seventeenth century. Arrival at London or Bristol was merely the last point, therefore, of a process of internal mobility; by the time emigrants arrived there they had presumably exhausted their possibilities for employment within the domestic economy. The best available option appeared to be to resettle in the colonies. The geographic mobility they had experienced in England made them familiar with packing up their clothes, travelling light, and tramping the roads for work. Already predisposed to being mobile, it may be that the decision to uproot themselves abroad was not so unsettling as was once supposed.

Very few indentured servants left written explanations of their motives for emigration; and, as with any individual or family intending to live abroad permanently, there were a myriad of possibilities, expectations and prospects to consider. But material factors were undoubtedly prominent in the minds of the servants emigrating to the Chesapeake; this was a secular migration without the religious impulse that impelled so many other migrants to flee England for New England during the seventeenth century. There may have been additional factors at work. Farley Grubb has shown that contracts recorded in London between 1682 and 1686 reveal a high incidence of fatherlessness among servants emigrating to the Chesapeake. One reason for their emigration appears to reside in the lack of family assistance they could tap while making the transition from adolescence to adulthood.[8] Whether this situation occurred with earlier indentured servant migrants is unknown: the Bristol list, for example, does not include data on the parents of those listed. A broader reason for the emigration of white servants has been made by David Eltis, who sees the flow of bonded labour as a response by young people to an opportunity to set themselves up as landowners, even on a modest scale. By such action they would achieve independence from the labour market and from stiff penalties against vagrancy and idleness in Stuart England. Given that such opportunities were unavailable to unskilled wage labourers in England through lack of funds, temporary servitude in America might not have seemed a bad option in circumstances where some form of dependency was common for young manual workers with few prospects.[9]

Ship captains also played a significant role in advertising berths on their vessels for servant migrants. Moreover, a broad range of people engaged in port and maritime activities participated in servant recruitment. For 1654 to 1660, 56 per cent of the Bristol masters sending servants to the Chesapeake were merchants and mariners; the remainder practised a wide range of urban trades. There was much speculation in shipping servants by small-scale tradesmen, something that also characterized the masters of indentured servants sent from London in

1682–6. The servant trade had no national regulation, though at Bristol during the Cromwellian protectorate the city's authorities regulated their flow, recording the details in the Tolzey Book. This resulted from the Bristol mercantile elite's desire to control interlopers in the trade. Henceforth indentures had to be taken out by small-scale shippers of servants who usually steered clear of such documents. By such means, established merchants could check the activities of lesser fry using the port. The fact that the Bristol servant registration list arose from specific local economic and political circumstances helps to explain why such record-keeping was unusual for seventeenth-century servants.

There were various means of recruiting servants. Promotional tracts for Virginia had been printed since the time of Richard Hakluyt. Lord Baltimore, the proprietor of Maryland, had published several pamphlets advertising his colony and its opportunities. Handbills, pamphlets and broadsides circulated in ports, proclaiming the material benefits that awaited emigrants in the New World. Some were written by migrants who had returned from the colonies. George Alsop, author of the *Character of the Province of Maryland*, had once been a servant in the colony and gave a positive view of Chesapeake society. 'What's a four years Servitude to advantage a man all the remainder of his dayes, making his predecessors happy in his sufficient abilities,' Alsop wrote, 'which he attained to partly by the restrainment of so small a time?' He added that servants in Maryland had 'the least cause to complain, either for strictness of Servitude, want of Provisions, or need of Apparel'. He noted that servants could claim an ancient privilege in the heat of the summer, whereby they rest indoors for three hours, and that they did little in the winter except cut wood to make fires.[10]

We do not know the extent to which prospective bonded labourers read these publications, but probably these printed items found their market more among entrepreneurs interested in America than among servants. Doubtless oral communication and persuasion played a larger part in inducing people to emigrate. Talk in inns and on the wharves and quays of English ports also helped to persuade some to sign up as indentured servants. There were shadowy recruiting agents known as 'spirits' who enticed people aboard ship. Little is known in detail about their activities. It may be that their role in procuring emigrant servants has been overplayed. Nonetheless, it is clear that they existed and that some were unscrupulous operators waiting to entrap the unwary and the vulnerable. Thus a Privy Council order of 1682 noted 'by reason of the frequent abuses of a lewd sort of People called Spirits in Seducing many of his Majtes subjects to go on shipboard where they have been seized and carried by force to his Majtes Plantacons in America' that 'many idle persons who have listed themselves voluntarily to be transported thither ... have afterwards pretended they were betrayed'.[11]

Most servant emigrants signed their indentures with the ship captain before embarkation, taking them out because they could not afford the £5 or £6 usually needed for the cost of passage to North America. But some went aboard ship without written documents. The former were sold for the lengths of their contracts to purchasers of their labour. The latter had arrangements made for them on arrival at their American destination according to the 'custom of the country'. Whether servants had an informed notion of what lay ahead of them before they boarded ship in London or Bristol and whether they could choose the colony to which they sailed are not entirely clear. The existence of propaganda literature and the various recruitment techniques outlined above indicate, at best, that hope played a large part in the decision; the tales of woe that sometimes filtered back from the colonies were not a sufficient disincentive for some.

Servant choice over destinations has attracted two opposing historical views. One stresses the lack of servant input into the decision, arguing that ship captains and their merchant masters added emigrants to ships destined for certain colonies with commodities already stowed on board. The other view, emphasizing the shorter length of servant contracts in the Caribbean than in the Chesapeake, suggests that bonded emigrants could select from a range of options, weighing up the economic advantages when making their choice. To some extent servants could bargain over their contracts; for a group leaving London in the 1680s who wrote their names on the indenture form signed up for a term seven months shorter than those who did not. This suggests that literacy was an advantage in taking out contracts. But in Bristol, and to a lesser extent in London, ships waiting on the quays for winds to carry them on their outward voyages had firm destinations agreed, and it is hard to believe that, if only vessels bound to the Caribbean were currently available for boarding, potential migrants would wait until a ship bound to Virginia or Maryland was rigged and cleared for departure. Shippers played the decisive role in the destination of ships carrying indentured servants – none of which, incidentally, were vessels purely for the shipment of people – and the fact that Virginia was the main colony in North America to which bonded servants were taken before 1660 doubtless reflected the incentives of the headright system for masters of vessels.

The Social Status of Servants

Descriptions of the social status of bonded emigrants have varied. Tracing the main contours of how this has evolved is an interesting exercise in the changing interpretation of an important issue in early American history. In a 1931 reprint of a piece originally written in 1913 Marcus W. Jernegan generalized, on the basis of little hard evidence, by stating that 'most of the servants were unskilled laborers, though many artisans and some in the professions bound themselves to service'.[12] In 1947 Abbot Emerson Smith, in a detailed study of servitude in America, echoed this judgement by characterizing bonded migrants as the riff-raff of Stuart England, as 'rogues, whores, vagabonds.' Such people, he contended, were largely unskilled labourers.'[13] This conclusion, also based on unsystematic evidence, reflected some of the negative contemporary descriptions of white servants. Typical examples are William Bullock writing in 1649 that many indentured servants came from among the country's 'idle, lazie, simple people,' and Governor William Berkeley complaining in 1662 that there was a scarcity of able workmen in Virginia 'for onely such servants as have been brought up to no art or Trade, hunger and fear of prisons bring to us.'[14]

In 1959 Mildred Campbell re-examined the social origins of these early Americans by focusing on the indentured servant records already described. Her investigation of the Bristol and London emigrant lists for 1654–86 and 1683–4 arrived at a different conclusion: yeomen and husbandmen predominated among the servants followed by artisans, tradesmen and labourers in descending numerical order. She used these findings to argue that the majority of the bonded servants migrating came from the middling ranks of the English population.[15] Her calculations assumed that the large number of male servants with no occupations recorded were a random sample of the whole; in other words, that they fitted the cross-section and distribution of groups that were recorded. This revisionist view of the status of seventeenth-century indentured servants was influential for almost twenty years.

In a convincing reinterpretation of the Bristol document, published in 1978, Galenson suggested that local officials were less conscientious about recording occupations after the first few years of registration, and that after 1657 they probably began to omit the descriptions of unskilled workers as labourers. He also argued that in seventeenth-century England, where hierarchical status was deeply embedded in society, it would have been unusual for a person's occupation to remain unrecorded. Though the data under scrutiny cover only a fragment of the total white servants going to America, they suggest that unskilled labourers were a more significant group than Campbell recognized. The conclusion drawn was that no single occupational group or level of status was found among these servants; rather, they comprised a cross-section of what contemporaries called the 'common sort' of people. In Galenson's words: 'A large number were farmers, both yeomen and husbandmen. Another sizable portion was made up of men skilled in a wide variety of trades and crafts ... A third substantial part was composed of those without such skills or fixed occupations, most of whom probably had worked for hire by the day in agriculture ... Finally, a significant group comprised the young men who had not yet entered independent positions in English society and who chose to complete their life-cycle service in America.'[16] This statement points up the varied nature of the servant outflow, indicating the broad swathe of social groups beneath the gentry from which they emanated. Further support for this conclusion is provided by evidence on the literacy of servants. Defining their literacy by their ability to sign the indentures, literacy rates for the servants included in the seventeenth-century lists are comparable with a regional sample for England for the 1680s. The servants were 'no less literate by occupation than their counterparts elsewhere in England' and those 'who recorded occupations were not disproportionately the least educated and skilled of those who practised their trades'.[17]

Master–Servant Relations

The absence of many surviving letters, account books and diaries, along with the predominance of oral communication, means that the social relations between masters and white servants are difficult to recapture. The best sources for looking at the interaction between the two groups are local court records in different colonies, a voluminous source mined extensively by the late Richard B. Morris.[18] Though one should be cautious in assuming that court records present a normative view of master–servant relations, owing to the simple fact that they mainly deal with disputes, they are still the best way of probing the tensions in an unequal social relationship. A summary account of the issues at stake in court cases will highlight the points of friction in labour relations and show the obligations of both parties and the matters over which they could seek redress. Indentured servants, because of the contractual nature of their employment, which legally regarded them as the chattel property of their owners, were subject in their action and behaviour to court decisions. Thus legal cases were the one crucial way in which they could regulate the behaviour of their superiors with whom they were in daily contact.

Statutes enacted and proclamations issued in Virginia and Maryland gave masters firm rights over their servant charges. Masters could inflict corporal punishment on recalcitrant bonded labourers. They could sell, assign or hire out servants, the unexpired term of the servant being the owner's property. They could dispose of indentured labourers in their wills, the workers being treated as part of a decedent master's estate. They could require servants to work six days a week in the tobacco fields. They had the backing of the law in dealing with servants who escaped. Anyone caught harbouring bonded fugitives in Maryland and Virginia was required to pay the master damages. A Virginia Act of 1659 stated that the hair of runaway servants should be cut close near their ears to identify them. In both Chesapeake colonies servants were forbidden to leave their homes without a licence or pass.

Penalties for servant runaways were stiff. A Maryland statute of 1641 made absconding from one's master, or helping another servant to escape, a felony punishable by death. Subsequent legislation in 1649 and 1661 dropped the capital sentence but substituted extra service for those caught after running away. The second of these two Acts specified ten days' extra service for each day spent at large. Some county courts, following the letter of the law, meted out thousands of days of additional service to returned fugitives. A Virginia Act of 1643 stipulated a double time for service for the first time a servant ran off. A later statute of 1668 permitted the master or magistrate to order corporal punishment as well as extra service. The usual sentence imposed by the General Court of Virginia was twenty to thirty-nine lashes (the upper limit being determined by biblical precedent in the Book of Deuteronomy and Corinthians). Another Virginian Act of 1705 made captured servants liable to serve one-and-a-half months for every 100lb of tobacco expended by their owners, and to recover costs rated at one year's service for 800lb tobacco.

Local courts in the Chesapeake, however, also provided considerable protection for servants' rights. By law masters had to provide appropriate living quarters for bonded workers; they could not make a second contract with servants who had completed their term; they were not allowed to overwork or ill-treat servants beyond the statutory stipulation, mentioned above, for corporal punishment in certain circumstances. Criminal prosecution ensued and fines were established for masters found guilty of overstepping these marks. The usual method of servants bringing their complaints to court was via petitions. They had full testimonial capacity, which gave them an advantage over servants who stayed in Britain, where such a situation was not allowed legally until 1747. Servants often succeeded in their claims brought before the courts for bad treatment over food, shelter or clothing. But risks had to be taken in order to enter court in the first place. Sometimes it was difficult to get witnesses to testify to the plaintiffs' accusations, especially when they relied, as frequently occurred, on the support of other servants. The fines given to masters were usually less severe than those handed down to servants when cases were decided. Typically, a master would be admonished or fined for bad behaviour and the acquitted servant assigned by the court to a new master. But when a servant was found guilty of false testimony, he or she could be whipped or ordered to serve for an additional three or six months with their original master.

Doubtless reasonably good master–servant relations prevailed where both sides recognized the obligations and limitations on their behaviour. But a significant number of cases involving abuse of servants surfaced in the courts. For example, in Maryland in 1659 the servant William Ireland accused his master Captain Philip Morgan of 'unhumanly' beating him, making him work at night, maltreating other servants in his charge, and not giving them sufficient to eat. The Provincial Court ordered Morgan to stop beating his servant, to release Ireland from night work, to let his servants work under reasonable conditions, and to provide them all with adequate food.[19] There were further examples of servants being treated badly. Dutch travellers in late seventeenth-century Maryland found that servants and slaves 'after they have worn themselves down the whole day, and gone home to rest, have yet to grind and pound the grain, which is generally maize, for their masters and all their families as well as themselves, and all the negroes, to eat'.[20] Few studies have concentrated directly on the work performed by seventeenth-century indentured servants, but the implication in the last example that their daily labour was arduous is confirmed by the finding that they worked an average day of 8–10 hours in the Chesapeake compared with the 6 hours normally performed by English field labourers.

Opportunities as Freedmen

The life history of Daniel Clocker indicates how an indentured servant could graduate, as it were, to a successful life in the New World. Born around 1619 in Cumberland, among the mountains and fells of north-west England, Clocker emigrated as an indentured servant, probably from London, in 1636. Little is known about his family background. On arrival in Maryland, he was bound as a servant to Thomas Cornwaleys, one of the Roman Catholic leaders of that colony. He probably helped to build the small town of St Mary's on the lower western shore of Maryland. His indenture ended in 1640. What he then did is unknown, but more information is available after his marriage to Mary Lawne Courtney, a widow with a young son, in either 1645 or 1646. He was clearly industrious, for in the 1650s he acquired 200 acres of land, sufficient to provide an inheritance for the five living children he and his wife had produced by 1661. The Clockers grew and sold tobacco. Daniel also worked as a carpenter, Mary as a dairymaid. He participated in community affairs, becoming a justice of the peace for St Mary's County in 1655, while she became the local midwife. Daniel briefly became a military officer in Maryland in 1660. He later took on voluntary positions in county and provincial affairs and became a member of the common council of St Mary's City. Predeceased by his wife, he died in 1676, leaving 230 acres and about £71 in movable property. As Lois Green Carr, who has reconstructed his career, concludes: 'Daniel Clocker had arrived in Maryland with nothing but the willingness and capacity to work with his hands; he died a well-respected land-owner who had served in a position of power, albeit briefly.'[21]

The extent to which Clocker's post-servant life typified the realization of opportunities available to early immigrants to the Chesapeake cannot be determined definitively. Only a comparatively small number of indentured servants can be traced throughout their life cycle in America and only a few worthwhile studies of this topic have been carried out. Older studies came to conflicting conclusions on opportunities for freedmen. Thomas J. Wertenbaker's investigation of Virginia's land books before 1666 concluded that between 30 and 40

per cent of the landholders of the colony had arrived under indenture.[22] Abbot Emerson Smith was less sanguine. His rule of thumb was
that about one in ten servants completed their indentures and gained
land plus some prosperity; a further one in ten became artisans but not
landowners; and eight in ten either died as servants, returned to
England, or became part of the underbelly of poor white workers in
the colonies.[23] These proportions, it should be noted, are mere hunches;
they rest on no statistical foundation and so, though cited frequently,
they should not be taken too seriously. There is also the assumption, in
Smith's account, that the 80 per cent of former Chesapeake servants
who did not acquire land or become tradesmen necessarily had to fend
in a difficult labour market to keep body and soul together. This ignores
the experience they would have gained learning agricultural techniques
and learning trades while they served in bondage and the possibilities of
tenancy or hired labour.

Opportunities for freedmen in Virginia appear to have been slim
after 1660. Poverty and early deaths were common. In Lancaster
County less than 10 per cent of the servants freed between 1662 and
1678 were householders by 1679. More detailed investigations of
seventeenth-century Maryland have illuminated the living standards
of freedmen in that colony. These studies are based on small numbers of
people, but they have tried to follow individuals from their point of
arriving in the Chesapeake Bay through to the point when they died: as
in the vignette of Clocker summarized above. They exclude detailed
consideration of women because marriage registers are unavailable for
the seventeenth-century Chesapeake, making it virtually impossible to
trace ex-female servants, who frequently married soon after attaining
their freedom. Perhaps the major theme to emerge from these investigations is that the potential opportunities for freed servants varied
over the course of the seventeenth century: the earlier immigrants
appear to have fared better than the later ones. Russell R. Menard's
study of all indentured servants who came to Maryland before 1642
found 275 men. Some 117 disappeared from the records before becoming free; most of them probably died. Of the remainder, 92 were still
living in Maryland ten or more years after gaining their freedom.
Ninety per cent of the 92 acquired land (but only 29 per cent of the
original sample) and 30 per cent gained political office, albeit briefly in
many cases. The main conclusion to be drawn here is that most of the
275 servants failed to live in Maryland sufficiently long to own land but

that opportunities were high for those who stayed there for at least a decade after their servant status ended.[24] Another study of a group of servants arriving in Maryland in the 1660s found that more than half who stayed on in the colony failed to achieve land as freemen, none acquired substantial wealth, and a smaller proportion than the earlier group were involved in government.[25] In the 1670s some ex-servants became tenant farmers or small planters, but opportunities declined for this group in Maryland in the last two decades of the seventeenth century. Given these findings, it is unsurprising that servants arriving in America from the 1680s onwards migrated to a wider range of colonies in search of better opportunities for the future after they had served out their indenture.

Notes

1. Quoted in Abbot Emerson Smith, *Colonists in Bondage: White Servitude and Convict Labor in America 1607–1776* (Chapel Hill: University of North Carolina Press, 1947), pp. 239–40.
2. Assembly Proceedings, 29 Mar. 1698, in William Hand Browne (ed.), *Archives of Maryland, vol. xxii: Proceedings and Acts of the General Assembly of Maryland March 1697/8 July 1699* (Baltimore, MD: Maryland Historical Society, 1902), p. 120.
3. Quoted in Susan M. Kingsbury (ed.), *Records of the Virginia Company of London*, 4 vols (Washington, DC: Government Printing Office, 1906–35), 3, p. 221.
4. British Library, Egerton MS 2,395, fo. 415b.
5. David Galenson, *White Servitude in Colonial America: An Economic Analysis* (Cambridge: Cambridge University Press, 1981); James Horn, 'Servant Emigration to the Chesapeake in the Seventeenth Century' in Thad W. Tate and David L. Ammerman (eds), *The Chesapeake in the Seventeenth Century: Essays on Anglo-American Society and Politics* (Chapel Hill: University of North Carolina Press, 1979), pp. 51–95; David Souden, '"Rogues, Whores and Vagabonds"? Indentured Servant Emigration to North America and the Case of Mid-Seventeenth Century Bristol', *Social History*, 3 (1978), pp. 23–41, reprinted in Peter Clark and David Souden (eds), *Migration and Society in Early Modern England* (London: Hutchinson, 1987), ch. 5.
6. Horn, 'Servant Emigration', p. 68.
7. Ibid., pp. 72–3.
8. Farley Grubb, 'Fatherless and Friendless: Factors influencing the Flow of English Emigrant Servants', *Journal of Economic History*, 52 (1992), pp. 85–108.
9. David Eltis, 'Slavery and Freedom in the Early Modern World' in Stanley L. Engerman (ed.), *Terms of Labor: Slavery, Serfdom, and Free Labor* (Stanford, CA: Stanford University Press, 1999), pp. 40–1.
10. George Alsop, *A Character of the Province of Maryland...* (1666; New York: repr. William Gowans, 1869), pp. 54–5, 57.
11. Quoted in Galenson, *White Servitude*, pp. 190–1.
12. Marcus W. Jernegan, *Laboring and Dependent Classes in Colonial America* (Chicago: University of Chicago Press, 1931), pp. 51–2.

13. Smith, *Colonists in Bondage*, p. 3.

14. William Bullock, *Virginia Impartially examined, and left to publick view, to be considered by all Judicious and honest men* (London, 1649), p. 14; William Berkeley, *A Discourse and View of Virginia* (London, 1662), p. 4.

15. Mildred Campbell, 'Social Origins of Some Early Americans' in James Morton Smith (ed.), *Seventeenth-Century America: Essays in Colonial History* (Chapel Hill: University of North Carolina Press, 1959), pp. 63–89.

16. David W. Galenson, '"Middling People" or "Common Sort"? The Social Origins of Some Early Americans Reexamined', *William and Mary Quarterly*, 3rd series, 35 (1978), pp. 499–524. See also Mildred Campbell, 'Response', ibid., pp. 525–40; Galenson, 'The Social Origins of Some Early Americans: A Rejoinder', ibid., 36 (1979), pp. 264–77; and Campbell, 'Reply', ibid., pp. 277–86.

17. Galenson, *White Servitude*, pp. 70–1.

18. Richard B. Morris, *Government and Labor in Early America* (New York: Columbia University Press, 1946), pp. 390–512.

19. Provincial Court, Patuxent, 22 Sept. 1657, in Browne (ed.), *Archives of Maryland*, vol. *xx: Judicial and Testamentary Business of the Provincial Court, 1649/50–1657* (Baltimore, MD: Maryland Historical Society, 1891), p. 521.

20. Henry C. Murphy (ed.), *Journal of a Voyage to New York and a Tour in Several of the American Colonies in 1679–80 by Jaspar Dankers and Peter Sluyter of Wiewerd in Friesland*, Memoirs of the Long Island Historical Society, 1 (Brooklyn, 1867), p. 216.

21. Lois Green Carr, 'Daniel Clocker's Adventure: From Servant to Freeholder' in Ian K. Steele and Nancy L. Rhoden (eds), *The Human Tradition in Colonial America* (Wilmington, DE: Scholarly Resources, Inc., 1999), pp. 97–118.

22. Thomas J. Wertenbaker, *The Planters of Colonial Virginia* (Princeton: Princeton University Press, 1922), pp. 75–80.

23. Smith, *Colonists in Bondage*, pp. 299–300.

24. Russell R. Menard, 'From Servant to Freeholder: Status Mobility and Property Accumulation in Seventeenth-Century Maryland', *William and Mary Quarterly*, 30 (1973), pp. 37–64.

25. Lois Green Carr and Russell R. Menard, 'Immigration and Opportunity: The Freedman in Early Colonial Maryland' in Tate and Ammerman (eds), *The Chesapeake in the Seventeenth Century*, pp. 206–42.

CHAPTER 2

From Servitude to Slavery

Indentured servitude and slavery predominated as labour institutions in those parts of seventeenth-century North America that came to be dominated by staple crop production on plantations. Though servants and slaves could be found in New England and the Middle Colonies, they were neither so numerous there nor so important for labour as in the southern colonies. But in the Chesapeake region, where tobacco production flourished from the 1620s, and in the Lower South, where rice cultivation predominated from the 1690s, both servants and slaves were extensively used. Moreover, in both these parts of the southern colonies a transition occurred from indentured white servants to slaves as the chief type of agricultural labourers. The timing of the transition from one mode of labour to another differed in South Carolina from Virginia; something that will be discussed below. But throughout the southern colonies the evolution of the labour market was closely tied to the need to maintain production levels in staple crops. Planters thereby could make profits and supply European markets with commodities such as tobacco and rice that were increasingly in demand there: tobacco as a luxury product that was processed in Europe into snuff or cut or roll tobacco for pipe-smoking, rice as a substitute commodity for basic food requirements when grain harvests were poor in the Iberian peninsula and northern Europe.

The initial choices available to English settlers to work the land in the Chesapeake consisted either in using white workers or in engaging or coercing Indian labour. The latter option was explored but proved unsuccessful. This was not because there were few Indians to exploit; quite the opposite in the early seventeenth century. Though population estimates for Native Americans are highly conjectural for this period, it seems that nearly a million Indians lived east of the Mississippi River on the eve of permanent English settlement. The number living in Virginia at this time could have been anything between 14,000 and 170,000, depending on whose estimates one follows. Whatever the numbers, the Indian presence in tidewater Virginia was of long duration by the 1620s;

at that time the Powhatan confederacy embraced about thirty groups of Indians living in that area. English settlers and Indians attempted to mediate the cultural gap between themselves by reciprocity over economic matters: white inhabitants wanted to cultivate and exploit land under Indian control, while Native Americans desired the manufactured goods that Englishmen brought with them from the mother country. But white settlers also tried to coopt Indian labour for agricultural production. This failed miserably for three main reasons: cultural differences, disease and conflict.

Indian ways of settlement and land cultivation proved inimical for the sort of agricultural production needed by whites in the Chesapeake. The Indians undertook subsistence agriculture and had their own rules about the use of land and natural resources, but these were different from English conceptions of property in land. Gatherers of beaver, wild turkey, deer and wampum from forests in hunting territories, and experienced catchers of fish at the water's edge, Native Americans were totally unused to the sort of labour required on plantations. In addition, their knowledge of the terrain meant that it would be difficult to contain them under such a system of land and crop cultivation. There was also a severe demographic problem. Epidemics occurred from time to time in which large numbers of Indians were devastated by tuberculosis, pneumonia, influenza, plague, measles, scarlet fever, smallpox and malaria – diseases that were partly the result of contact with people from a different disease environment. Many English settlers had experienced these ailments as children before crossing the Atlantic and were thus immune to them; but native communities could be swiftly decimated by contact with the carriers of these diseases.

The most important reason why Indians could not be coerced to work permanently by Europeans lay in the white man's view of Native Americans as uncivilized savages controlling land that was ripe for the picking. White settlers regarded themselves as culturally superior and saw the land as freely available. Indian resistance to white encroachments spilled over into violent encounters on several occasions in the seventeenth-century Chesapeake. In March 1622 Opechancanough, leader of the Powhatans, led an attack on the English to end the settlers' invasion of their world. This resulted in the death of 347 colonists. Transplanted Englishmen avenged the deaths of their compatriots by ambushing and killing Indians. In 1644 the Powhatans rose up against the English settlers in Virginia again, but this revolt was suppressed. A peace treaty was signed in October 1646. The Indian tribes remained in a weak position in Virginia for the next thirty years. In 1676, however, some Indians took up arms against the English in Bacon's Rebellion. Nathaniel Bacon, the organizer of the uprising, ordered his forces to kill some captured Occaneechees and to murder a group of Susquehannocks. Elsewhere in North America there were similar barbarous conflicts between Native Americans and white settlers, notably in the Pequot war (1636–7) and King Philip's war (1675–6) in New England. Such outbreaks of armed conflict did not stop all trade and exchange between Indians and English settlers but they signalled the failure of policies to subjugate Native Americans to the white man's dominance. There were, of course, exceptions. In 1708, for instance, some 1,400 Indians were held in bondage by South Carolina planters; they constituted about a third of the colony's population and had been mainly rounded up from conflicts between Native American groups in the south-east. One can also find occasional Indian workers on Chesapeake tobacco plantations. Nevertheless, Indian slavery declined in the Palmetto province from the early eighteenth century onwards, and few Native Americans could be found on Chesapeake tobacco estates by the same period.

James Axtell has raised some counterfactual speculations about how the development of British North America would have differed if there had been no Indians. In particular, he has suggested that black slavery would have spread more quickly in the Chesapeake and would have been more difficult to regulate without the presence of Native Americans. Thus a colonial America without Indians would have precipitated an earlier use of black slave labour in the Chesapeake because, in fact, it took time for white settlers to find that enslaving Indians did not work. With virgin land available at cheap prices, this counterfactual scenario implies that settlers would have bought land more easily, enabling them to pay for more enslaved Africans. At the same time, without Indians surrounding the border areas of plantations, it would have been more difficult for whites to keep the black population in check, for there would be no Indian slave catchers.[1] These speculations remind us that recourse to black slave labour *en masse* in the seventeenth-century Chesapeake was not the first solution to a labour shortage that settlers looked for or thought feasible. But it was not merely experiments with Indian labour that delayed the introduction of a large-scale black workforce; it also resulted from trying to create a white man's society in the Chesapeake and finding that, in terms of work, this again led to failure.

The Impact of the Atlantic Slave Trade

The eventual solution to the supply of labour for North American plantations lay via the Atlantic slave trade. The origins of this traffic stemmed from 1444, when the Portuguese landed an African cargo near Lagos on the Algarve. It lasted until the 1880s when Brazilian and Cuban slavery collapsed. For over four centuries seven European powers had a flourishing slave trade, with the Portuguese and Spanish pioneering the traffic in the fifteenth and sixteenth centuries and the English, French, Dutch and Danish following suit in the seventeenth century. The total number of captives shipped via the Atlantic slave trade is a hotly disputed matter, but most modern historians suggest that something in the region of 12 million Africans crossed the Atlantic during the entire period of the slave trade. Though this is a more modest total than some older studies suggested, it still represents a massive flow of people. It constitutes the largest inter-continental migration of men and women, whether free or enforced, in the early modern era. The British colonies in North America were thus the recipients of large numbers of people who were primarily bought as workers. They followed in the footsteps of what other European powers had already begun to exploit on a large scale for generations.

The first shipment of blacks, comprising twenty or more people, arrived in Virginia in 1619 aboard a Dutch man-of-war. But before 1660 the number of Africans in the North American population was relatively small. Indeed, in that period most slaves taken on English vessels were sent to Barbados; the total number shipped was probably about 10,000. After the Restoration of the Stuart monarchy, the slave trade grew rapidly. Between 1662 and 1670 some 59,900 slaves were put aboard English and colonial vessels in Africa. Annual shipments of slaves by the English rose sixfold in the ensuing century. Over the entire period from 1662 to 1807 about 3.4 million slaves were carried to different parts of the British Empire. The majority of Africans taken by English slave traders always ended up in the Caribbean, but the southern colonies of British North America were important secondary markets. This is reflected in the black population figures given in Table 2.1 and in estimates of the percentage of African-Americans in the total population of British America. In 1660 some 42 per cent of the

Table 2.1 Estimated black population of regions in British North America, 1620–1720

Year	New England	Middle Colonies	Chesapeake	Lower South
1620	0	0	–	–
1630	0	0	100	–
1640	200	200	100	–
1650	400	500	300	–
1660	600	600	900	0
1670	400	800	2,500	200
1680	500	1,500	4,300	400
1690	1,000	2,500	7,300	1,800
1700	1,700	3,700	12,900	2,900
1710	2,600	6,200	22,400	6,600
1720	4,000	10,800	30,600	14,800

Source: John J. McCusker and Russell R. Menard, *The Economy of British America, 1607–1789* (Chapel Hill: University of North Carolina Press, 1985), pp. 103, 136, 172, 203.

British West Indian population was black; by 1700 the proportion was 78 per cent. In 1660 the proportion of African-Americans in the different British North American regions was under 2 per cent for New England, 11.5 per cent for the Middle Colonies, 3.6 per cent for the Chesapeake and 2 per cent for the Lower South. By 1700 the black portion of the population was less than 2 per cent for New England, 7 per cent for the Middle Colonies, 13 per cent for the Chesapeake, and 17 per cent for the Lower South. Shortly afterwards, around 1710, South Carolina became the first British colony in North America to have a black majority in its population.

  The escalation of the British slave trade in the four decades after 1660 explains the growth of the black population in the southern American colonies in that period. In 1660 the Company of Royal Adventurers to Africa, based in London, began trading to the coast of west Africa in search of gold, mainly from the Senegal River down to the Bight of Benin. It soon found that purchasing slaves from local black traders was a more reliable and lucrative source of profit, for enslaved Africans could be sold profitably in the New World. The Company of Royal Adventurers to Africa was succeeded in 1672 by another joint-stock company based in the metropolis. This was the Royal African Company, an organization that held a monopoly in the English slave trade until 1698, when King William III supported a parliamentary Act that opened the trade to private merchants as well. Before 1698 London dominated the English slave trade because it was the headquarters of the Royal African Company. Thereafter private merchants from London, Bristol and Liverpool were prominent in the trade.

The Royal African Company built forts and castles on the west African coast, in areas such as the Gambia, to store goods and to protect their officials and slave captives. They operated the famous triangular trade that was a hallmark of all transatlantic slaving. Under this system, ships sailed on the first leg of their voyage from an English port with goods such as textile and metalware to barter or sell for slaves in Africa. After purchasing slaves in west Africa the vessels embarked on the second leg of the voyage across the Atlantic. This was known as the 'Middle Passage.' Slaves were chained and stowed in ships' holds, being only allowed up on deck for brief periods during the day for food and exercise. The Middle Passage ended with the delivery of slaves to an appropriate market in the West Indies or North America. The slaves were sold, often on shipboard, to purchasers who bought their black charges for their lifetime, with the prospect of their offspring being born into slavery. The third and final leg of the voyage consisted of slave vessels loading tropical or semi-tropical produce for the voyage home and the prospect of a third set of profits from their sale in England. Though lengthy slaving voyages lasting more than a calendar year were a risky form of commercial enterprise, they offered better opportunity costs to investors than putting money into safer investments such as government funds. This is reflected in contemporary discussions of the lucre to be gained from slave trading. Thus the English writer on trade John Cary, in a classic mercantilist text, waxed enthusiastically about the Guinea traffic as 'a Trade of the most Advantage to this Kingdom of any we drive'.[2]

The Reasons for Enslavement

The large-scale adoption of slave labour owed much to the growth of the English slave trade after 1660, but it was not simply a question of more regular supply of enslaved Africans that triggered the beginning of the racial transformation of the North American population. Social and cultural reasons for enslaving Africans also assumed significance. English attitudes towards Africans in the seventeenth century partly reflected a widespread ethnocentrism and xenophobia towards 'others'.

There is plenty of evidence that Englishmen regarded Jews with suspicion and that diverse groups such as Irish Catholics and Scottish Highlanders were often regarded with hostility or downright hatred. And yet none of these groups were enslaved. Thus the other cultural reason for the enslavement of Africans was something more than just ethnocentrism: it consisted of racial prejudice towards black Africans. Blackness, in terms of skin colour, had negative connotations for not just the British but many Europeans in the early modern era (though these associations were probably less marked in Portugal and Spain where there had been a longer tradition of regular contact with African people). Blackness, for Stuart people, suggested connections with the Devil. A leading English imperialist of the early seventeenth century, intimately involved with the Virginia colony, summarized this view. 'Negroes in Africa', wrote Captain John Smith, 'bee as idle and as devilish people as any in the world.'[3] Africans were also associated with Noah's curse on the son of Ham. George Sandys, an official of the Virginia Company, noted that African slaves were 'descended of Chus, the sonne of the cursed Cam; as are all of that complexion'.[4] Africans were known to be heathens, something that made them seem barbaric to many western Europeans. They were feared for their lust and savagery. Africans were also singled out for their sheer difference from Europeans: in their physiognomy, gestures, languages, dress and behaviour. Together, an amalgam of negative attitudes emerged that constituted racial prejudice towards Africans.

Such attitudes were underpinned by the widespread tolerance of slavery by Europeans in the seventeenth century. European trading nations with empires knew that slavery had existed in human societies since ancient times; that various passages in Scripture condoned the existence of slave societies; and that the educated classes widely accepted the practice of slavery. Though some dissenting voices were troubled about the moral implications of enslaving other people, notable European jurists such as Hugo Grotius and John Selden did not question the existence of slavery. Two leading English philosophers of the late seventeenth century also accepted slavery as if it were a normal feature of society. Thomas Hobbes in *Leviathan* viewed slavery as part of the world's system of subordination and authority. For him, a system of law and power had partly replaced the divine order, and, within the new dispensation, slavery was a rational and harmonious component. John Locke, the philosopher of liberty, stressed the nature of contractual obligations between rulers and ruled, and the natural right of the ruled to withdraw their consent when governed in an unjust manner; but within this contract theory he could find no room for slavery. Indeed, his actions indicated an acceptance of slavery, for he was a shareholder in the Royal African Company. The reason why advocates of natural-rights theories condoned enslavement appears to have lain in their acceptance of slavery as a flourishing African institution, for it should not be forgotten that slaves were a major form of wealth in Africa and that an Islamic slave trade had flourished there for centuries before European slave traders participated in the traffic. In other words, European intellectuals could have a clear conscience about slave trading because Africans had already bartered away their liberty before they came into the hands of ship captains on the west African coast.

Negative perceptions of black Africans coupled with a virtually non-existent anti-slavery posture created the cultural outlook whereby European traders and New World settlers were morally untroubled in enslaving black human beings. But another aspect of the general matrix of white racial superiority should also be added. This was the importance of freedom in English society and the lack of examples of permanent bondage found therein. Englishmen prided themselves on the fact that they were free-born Englishmen with legal rights at common law. Even indentured servants, despite their lowly status, had access to the law courts and hence the means to challenge any treatment of them that they considered unlawful. Evidence from the seventeenth-century Chesapeake indicates that their rights were often upheld in courts when they were in dispute with their masters. There was no tradition of permanent bondage in English society, nothing equivalent to the serfdom that was deeply embedded in Russia and other eastern European societies for centuries. Serfdom, of course, was an enforced labour system like slavery, though it was not so frequently tied to large agricultural holdings. The fact that neither serfdom nor slavery flourished on English soil meant that bonded labour at home avoided chattel status and the concomitant absence of legal rights. But though slavery was not a condition found in England, one should add that legal decisions in 1693 and 1696 left its status in England in an equivocal position.

English attitudes towards black Africans and slavery were important influences lying behind the acceptance of slaveholding in the seventeenth-century Chesapeake and Carolinas. Whether racial prejudice preceded slavery in North America or whether it escalated when large numbers of Africans were imported regularly has led, however, to disagreement among historians. Some scholars consider that the various reasons outlined above for the debasement of blacks were sufficient for their large-scale enslavement when the opportunity arose to do so with the growth of the English slave trade. In other words, racial prejudice was a sufficiently ingrained trait to justify shipping millions of Africans to the New World via the Middle Passage. This view supports Winthrop D. Jordan's notion of an 'unthinking decision' in enslaving Africans – something so deeply embedded in the traders that it operated at almost a subconscious level.[5] Yet other historians are not convinced that the various attitudes that singled out blacks for degradation are enough to explain the origins of North American slavery. They point out that the treatment of blacks and their interaction with whites and Native Americans varied considerably over time. Ira Berlin, for instance, has recently popularized the notion of communities of Atlantic creoles, living in the port communities on Atlantic shores, sometimes in Africa, sometimes in the Americas; they acted as trade and cultural brokers without great interference or debasement from whites and only some ended up as slaves. The social relations between Atlantic creoles and European traders and settlers were more flexible than found in slave societies based on plantation labour.[6]

The debate over the origins of North American slavery has long generated discussion with regard to seventeenth-century Virginia. In an important article published in 1950, Oscar and Mary Handlin suggested that racial prejudice was not an important factor in the treatment of slaves in North America – and that means blacks primarily in the Chesapeake – before 1660. Noting that the term 'slave' was used in a fluid fashion before that date to refer to Indians, mulattoes and the servitude of white children as much as to Africans, they argued that slaves were treated as servants before the mid-seventeenth century and that chattel status of slaves, fastening them to hereditary bondage as the property of white people, only came thereafter with the rapid importation of slaves to Virginia and Maryland. The Handlins further argued that the legal status of chattel slaves only arose when tobacco planters attempted to attract voluntary white workers by debasing the condition of involuntary black labour. Only after that occurred did racial prejudice become an important factor in the treatment of enslaved Africans in America.[7] Others responded to these arguments from a different perspective. Carl N. Degler was one notable critic of the Handlins' views. He argued that racism existed from the moment that blacks stepped ashore in Virginia, and that what the Handlins regarded as the worsening status of blacks as they became legally defined as chattel was the codification of existing practices. Degler cited plenty of evidence to show that blacks were discriminated against in the Chesapeake even when the word 'slave' was not used in documents.[8] Others have suggested that the very fact that blacks in the Chesapeake were widely referred to as 'Negroes' set them apart from the white dependent class.

Defects in the surviving documentation make it difficult to resolve these opposing viewpoints. From 1619 until about 1640, insufficient documentary material survives to state categorically whether slaves were treated as servants or not. In the 1640s and 1650s, however, examples of the central feature of black slavery – hereditary lifetime service – can be found in Virginia. But if the Handlins were wrong to omit these references from their arguments, they were correct about the deteriorating status of slaves after 1660. In 1639 an Act of the Virginia Assembly singled out blacks for special treatment by stating that 'all persons except negroes' should be armed. One legal case of 1641 and two official actions of 1656 demonstrated that the black's position was deteriorating in the Old Dominion. But it was not until 1661 that perpetual bondage for blacks in Virginia received statutory recognition and not until 1669 that the Negro servant was designated as a chattel rather than as someone whose labour was just the property of his master. Rather than arguing, in a crude fashion, that either chattel slave status increased the propensity for racism among white Virginians or that racial prejudice determined the treatment of Africans from 1619 onwards, it is probably more accurate to demonstrate the gradual deterioration of the status of blacks as documents codified white–black relationships more explicitly. It is hard to believe that racial attitudes did not play a significant part in enslaving Africans, just as it is difficult to accept that such views alone were sufficient to sustain the Atlantic slave trade. But to suggest that a widespread number of those who purchased slaves were necessarily imbued with a deep-seated racial prejudice, and that this was their predominant motive for acquiring enslaved black workers, cannot be proven. One also needs to investigate the economic opportunities and development of plantations in the southern American colonies to understand the widespread adoption of slave labour in North America.

From Servitude to Slavery in the Chesapeake

The transition from servitude to slavery in the Chesapeake occurred in the four decades between 1680 and 1720. In the 1680s an increased number of slaves became available to Virginia and Maryland, while the supply of indentured servants had already declined. During the 1690s blacks became the majority of arrivals among immigrants to the Chesapeake for the first time. Nevertheless, it still took a couple of decades for slavery to become prominent in that region. Adopting Philip D. Morgan's criterion that slaveowning societies only became transformed into slave societies when the black proportion of the population reached 20 per cent, then Virginia only made the transition by 1710 and Maryland by 1720.[9] The regional distribution of slaves varied, however, within each colony. Generally in the tidewater areas, where the best quality tobacco was produced, between 30 and 40 per cent of the population consisted of slaves at the beginning of the eighteenth century. Once the transition from white servants to slaves had occurred, further African arrivals and strong reproductive rates among the black population meant that the Chesapeake became ever more committed to slavery: by 1750 some 40 per cent of the African-Americans in the thirteen British mainland colonies lived in that region.

Accounting for the transition from the predominant use of servant labour to the deployment of slave work in Virginia and Maryland during the late seventeenth and early eighteenth centuries is a complex matter. But several notions about how it occurred can be discarded. First, it is important to recognize that slave plantation labour was not vital to tobacco cultivation. Tobacco was a delicate crop that could be grown on small farms or quarters, often with a relatively small workforce of less than fifteen or twenty individuals. There were many small white farmers in Virginia cultivating tobacco. It was not necessary to grow the leaf on plantations. Slaves had no prior knowledge of tobacco cultivation from their home communities in west Africa. (As discussed below, a different situation obtained, it could be argued, with African skill in cultivating rice in the Carolina Lowcountry.) Second, the suggestion that less workers were needed in the Chesapeake by the 1680s because mortality had declined in that region by that decade is also implausible: the drop in mortality levels had already occurred by the 1660s and immigrant workers were as much sought after in the 1680s as they had been earlier in the century.

Some historians have argued that the transition from servitude to slavery in Virginia began just a few years after Bacon's Rebellion rocked the social fabric of white society, and that the demand for greater imports of blacks reflected fears in the Chesapeake about the white underclass. Edmund S. Morgan in particular has argued that Bacon's Rebellion (discussed in Chapter 5) had a significant impact on the greater importation of slaves rather than servants in the Chesapeake region from the 1680s onwards.[10] This contention is difficult to prove even though the social dissatisfaction that caused the revolt had hardly withered by the 1680s when tobacco prices were stagnant and economic depression hit the tobacco industry in Virginia and Maryland. A simpler reason for finding Morgan's argument unconvincing, however, is that the supply of indentured servants to the Chesapeake had dried up in the years immediately following the disturbance of the 1670s: even if Virginia farmers and planters had wanted to continue purchasing white servants at that time, the number of indentured migrants was insufficient to meet their needs.

The best explanations of the transition from servitude to slavery in the Chesapeake, associated primarily with the work of David Galenson and Russell R. Menard, emphasize the changing supply and demand situation for servants at this time plus the increased availability of African slaves, who were obtainable via the Royal African Company's ships in conditions of nearly perfect elasticity of supply.[11] These related phenomena, it should be noted, did not exactly coincide in time. The availability of new indentured servants had tapered off significantly since 1660. It continued to decline until the late 1670s, when the flow became a trickle. Large importations of slaves to the Chesapeake only began in the 1680s – both directly from Africa and from the West Indies – but it was not until the first decade of the eighteenth century that the supply of Africans to Virginia and Maryland was regular. Thus the rise of slavery in the Chesapeake was a consequence, not a cause, of the decrease in the availability of white bonded labour.

The fall in the supply of white servants partly stemmed from changing social, economic and demographic conditions in the mother country. English population growth was stagnant in the last half of the seventeenth century. This meant that there was not so much pressure on subsistence levels as there had been among the labouring poor before the Stuart Restoration. Wages improved for ordinary workers and there was less geographic mobility among the English population; where mobility occurred it was usually over fairly short distances such as ten or fifteen miles. In general, the reasons why a young adult might become mobile in search of better opportunities were less evident than earlier in the century. Thus a sequence of two or three, possibly more, removals within England before migrants arrived at a port and decided to ship themselves across the ocean with an indenture was less common. Net emigration figures support these points. England produced 100,000 net emigrants in the 1640s, 100,000 in the 1660s, 40,000 in the 1680s and 50,000 in the 1700s. In addition, pressures existed at home for the government to retain population in the late seventeenth century. 'There is nothing so much wanting in England as people,' one commentator averred, 'and all sorts of people, the industrious and laborious sort, and handicraftmen, are wanted to till and improve our land, and help to manufacture the staple commodites of the kingdom; which would add greatly to the riches thereof.'[12] This sentiment was echoed by many other writers of the time.

Of course, indentured servants still crossed the ocean in the 1680s and 1690s. But by that period they had a wider choice of destination than had been the case earlier in the century. Whereas before the English Civil War and Interregnum the main settlements available for indentured servants in the Americas were the Chesapeake and Caribbean colonies, by the reigns of Charles II and James II additional settlements such as the Carolinas, East and West Jersey, and Pennsylvania attracted immigrants and were promoted in colonization literature. Some English indentured servants still found their way to Virginia and Maryland in the late seventeenth century. They largely consisted of a higher proportion of women and adolescent boys, as well as children of the poor, than had been the case earlier. But many others went to the newer colonies settled after 1660. For instance, one-third of the 8,000 settlers who flocked to Pennsylvania between 1681 and 1685, in the first large migration to William Penn's Quaker colony, were indentured servants. Their flow was augmented by a large influx of Irish servants and German redemptioners, as Chapter 3 will show. This trend towards a wider range of American destinations for servants and a more heterogeneous ethnic mix continued after 1700, and was one of the chief differences between the seventeenth- and eighteenth-century indentured migrants to British North America.

During the transition from servitude to slavery in the Chesapeake, comparative prices for both forms of labour played their part in determining planters' decisions to purchase unfree workers. This is not to reduce the switch from one form of labour to another to the level of price determinants only; that would be too reductionist an approach to the complex reasons for enslavement. Even so, purchasers acted in an economically rational manner. A fall in the supply of servants drove their price up. Whereas in Virginia and Maryland probate inventories slaves were valued at three times the price of white servants in the mid-1670s, the ratio had fallen to less than two-to-one by 1690. Given that tobacco prices were low in the 1680s and 1690s, available income for Chesapeake planters to purchase new labourers was tight. Indeed, it might be thought that stagnation in the tobacco industry between 1680 and 1715 would have deterred them from purchasing extra labourers, be they black or white. That this was not the case stemmed from the uneven regional impact of the depression along the tobacco coast: in tidewater localities producing good tobacco for European markets – areas such as the York and James River peninsulas in Virginia and Maryland's lower western shore – buying new slaves offered the prospects of better productivity and higher profits.

By 1690 servant prices were relatively high compared with slave prices (which were low in the 1680s because of the decline in sugar prices and sugar production in the Caribbean). Servants now usually had contracts only for four years (rather than seven earlier in the century) while slaves could be purchased for life and their offspring perpetuated through hereditary bondage. Thus it was not surprising that planters increasingly sought the use of slave labour even though there might have been doubts about the readiness of Africans to assimilate to new work routines and to prove, through work productivity, that they were in fact the better investment. The widespread purchase of enslaved Africans, in turn, was undoubtedly bolstered by the racial prejudice towards black people that we have already identified as part of white settlers' ethnocentrism in the seventeenth century. The shift from servant to slave labour in the Chesapeake involved, as Galenson has demonstrated, a reallocation to some degree of tasks so that whites performed more skilled labour, often of a supervisory nature, and blacks did the unskilled work in the tobacco fields.[13]

From Servitude to Slavery in South Carolina

The transition from servitude to slavery in South Carolina occurred rapidly after rice production began to dominate the colony's economy after 1690. Founded in 1670 as a proprietary province, South Carolina's economy was based initially on grazing cattle and cutting lumber, with a mixed workforce of free white labourers, indentured servants, Indians and some slaves. A fuller use of slave labour could have eventuated at the outset of the colony's history: the Proprietors of South Carolina made slavery legal in order to attract settlers; and strong connections were soon struck up, in terms of trade and settlement, between South Carolina and Barbados, where slave plantation labour had been used for several decades before the Carolinas were settled by whites. A quick transition from a mixed economy and labour force to one based on black gang labour on rice plantations in the swampy areas of the South Carolina Lowcountry proceeded rapidly after the successful cultivation of rice as an export staple crop occurred in the decades on either side of the turn of the eighteenth century. The shift from servitude to slavery in South Carolina was already evident by 1703. By 1721, when South Carolina became a royal colony, rice production had secured the rise of a class of wealthy planters and black slaves dominated the colony's labour force. The slave population of South Carolina rose from 2,400 in 1700 to 5,000 in 1710 to 12,000 in 1720 and to 22,700 in 1730: roughly a doubling of numbers in every decade. Small wonder that in 1737 a new immigrant to the colony remarked that South Carolina seemed 'more like a negro country than like a country settled by white people'.[14]

Between the 1670s and the 1690s, as Menard has shown, indentured servants were never as numerous in South Carolina as they had been earlier in Virginia and Maryland.[15] The chief reason lay in the declining supply of such servants in the late seventeenth century as a result of stagnant population growth and better wages and opportunities at home – the same reasons as discussed above for the falling supply of servants to the Chesapeake in the last quarter of the seventeenth century. Of the servants that South Carolina did attract, probably a third were migrants from the Caribbean. But free white men also did not supply widespread manual labour at this time because land prices were relatively cheap in South Carolina and it was not particularly difficult for an industrious white emigrant to acquire land and thereby enter the yeoman class. Once naval stores such as pitch, tar and turpentine had proved a profitable export and rice had been introduced as a staple crop there was an incentive for slave traders to send their ships to Charles Town, the principal port of South Carolina, in search of profitable sales. Initially many of these vessels came via the West Indies to

South Carolina. After that occurred – and it was in train by 1700 – South Carolina planters quickly purchased Africans for their plantations. In doing so, many were undoubtedly influenced by their West Indian experience of slavery. It was not difficult to justify the deployment of African labour in the swampy Lowcountry when coercion, discipline and legal codes that discriminated against blacks had already been practised by planters who had previously cultivated Caribbean sugar. In 1696 South Carolina enacted a slave code based on Barbadian precedents.

The growth in planting rice as a staple crop coincided with a regular supply of 'new negroes' or 'saltwater' slaves, as Africans arriving in America were termed, in a situation where the supply of indentured servants was sporadic. Thus the transition to slave labour in South Carolina did not pass through the protracted phase that had occurred earlier in the Chesapeake where a staple crop (tobacco) was being cultivated, plenty of indentured servants were initially available, few slaves were being imported, and therefore the attempt to use whites as a plantation labour force lasted for some time. In South Carolina a swifter process occurred: servants were difficult to acquire, African slaves were readily available, and, as in the Chesapeake, Indians were not enslaved on a large scale. The possibility of using Indians as slaves was potentially viable, however, in South Carolina. Figures have already been cited to indicate the extent of Indian slavery in South Carolina by c. 1700. But the situation changed thereafter. A sharp demographic decline occurred in the Indian population of the colony, in which several smaller tribes were totally destroyed. The Yamasee War of 1715–17, in which the Yamasees were deserted by their Indian allies and attacked by Cherokees, caused significant loss to life and property. Some Indian tribes also quit South Carolina in the early eighteenth century.

Purchasing enslaved Africans for plantation labour held certain drawbacks to Carolinians in the late seventeenth century: high prices for blacks could be a problem and the hard work to which bonded workers were subjected could lead to runaways. But the Africans had an additional attraction for buyers: namely their familiarity with rice cultivation, something explored in depth by Peter H. Wood and Daniel C. Littlefield.[16] European immigrants to the American colonies and Indians had little familiarity with sowing rice. But rice was a staple crop in the rain forests of the sub-Sahara region of west Africa and the part of the Windward coast where rice was especially cultivated was known as the Grain Coast. Some slave arrivals were familiar with growing rice in paddies along river banks in Africa, and experienced in the planting, hoeing, threshing, winnowing and cooking of the crop. Indeed, parallels have been found between the mortar-and-pestle technique of processing rice in parts of Africa and similar practices followed by slaves in eighteenth-century South Carolina. It may be that an additional reason, then, for the adoption of slave labour in that colony was the prior skills in rice cultivation brought by some Africans across the ocean; this would help to explain the joint growth of slavery and rice production in South Carolina between the 1690s and 1720s and the switch by planters from cultivating rice on dry land to using freshwater swamps. On the other hand, this part of the explanation about the transition from servitude to slavery in South Carolina can be challenged. Philip D. Morgan has raised some pertinent points on this matter. He notes that the coastal regions that mainly supplied Africans to South Carolina – notably Angola – were not rice-growing areas. Women were the main growers of rice in Africa, whereas the slave trade to Charleston was dominated by men. The type of rice grown in west Africa was cultivated in dry, upland areas, yet the Lowcountry rice plantation was generally situated in low-lying swampy areas requiring irrigation.[17] These caveats suggest that we should be circumspect in according to African practice the chief impetus behind the cultivation of rice in North America, though they do not deny that some Africans did possess prior skills that enabled them to adapt to working in South Carolina.

Notes

1. James Axtell, *After Columbus: Essays in the Ethnohistory of Colonial North America* (New York: Oxford University Press, 1988), pp. 234–5.
2. John Cary, *Essay on the State of England in relation to its Trade, its Poor and its Taxes, for carrying on the Present war against France* (1695), p. 74.
3. Philip L. Barbour (ed.), *The Complete Works of Captain John Smith [1580–1631]*, 3 vols (Chapel Hill: University of North Carolina Press, 1986), i, p. 327, iii, pp. 293–4.
4. George Sandys, *A Relation of a Journey Begun An: Dom: 1610*, 2nd edn (London, 1621), p. 136.
5. Winthrop D. Jordan, *White over Black: American Attitudes toward the Negro, 1550–1812* (Chapel Hill: University of North Carolina Press, 1968), ch. 2.
6. Ira Berlin, *Many Thousands Gone: The First Two Centuries of Slavery in North America* (Cambridge, MA: The Belknap Press of Harvard University Press, 1998), ch. 1.
7. Oscar and Mary F. Handlin, 'Origins of the Southern Labor System', *William and Mary Quarterly*, 7 (1950), pp. 199–222.

8. Carl N. Degler, 'Slavery and the Genesis of American Race Prejudice', *Comparative Studies in Society and History*, 2 (1959), pp. 49–66.

9. Philip D. Morgan, 'British Encounters with Africans and African-Americans, circa 1600–1780' in Bernard Bailyn and Philip D. Morgan (eds), *Strangers within the Realm: Cultural Margins of the First British Empire* (Chapel Hill: University of North Carolina Press, 1991), p. 163.

10. Edmund S. Morgan, *American Slavery, American Freedom: The Ordeal of Colonial Virginia* (New York: W. W. Norton, 1975), ch. 13. Cf. T. H. Breen, 'A Changing Labor Force and Race Relations in Virginia, 1660–1710' in his *Puritans and Adventurers: Change and Persistence in Early America* (New York: Oxford University Press, 1980), pp. 127–47.

11. David Galenson, *White Servitude in Colonial America: An economic analysis* (Cambridge: Cambridge University Press, 1981), esp. pp. 151–7, and 'Economic Aspects of the Growth of Slavery in the Seventeenth-Century Chesapeake' in Barbara L. Solow (ed.), *Slavery and the Rise of the Atlantic System* (New York: Cambridge University Press, 1991), pp. 265–92; Russell R. Menard, 'From Servants to Slaves: The Transformation of the Chesapeake Labor System', *Southern Studies*, 16 (1977), pp. 355–90.

12. Carew Reynel, *The True English Interest, or, An Account of the chief national improvements ...* (London, 1674), p. 54.

13. Galenson, *White Servitude in Colonial America*, pp. 159–60.

14. 'Samuel Dyssli to His Mother, Brother and Friends', 3 Dec. 1737, in R. W. Kelsey, 'Swiss Settlers in South Carolina', *South Carolina Historical and Genealogical Magazine*, 23 (1922), p. 90.

15. Russell R. Menard, 'The Africanization of the Lowcountry Labor Force' in Winthrop D. Jordan and Sheila L. Skemp (eds), *Race and Family in the Colonial South* (Jackson, MS: University of Mississippi Press, 1987), pp. 81–108.

16. Peter H. Wood, *Black Majority: Negroes in Colonial South Carolina from 1670 through the Stono Rebellion* (New York: A. A. Knopf, 1974), pp. 35–62; Daniel C. Littlefield, *Rice and Slaves: Ethnicity and the Slave Trade in Colonial South Carolina* (Baton Rouge: Louisiana State University Press, 1981), pp. 44–114.

17. Philip D. Morgan, *Slave Counterpoint: Black Culture in the Eighteenth-Century Chesapeake and Lowcountry* (Chapel Hill: University of North Carolina Press, 1998), pp. 182–3.

CHAPTER 3

Convicts, Indentured Servants and Redemptioners, 1680–1775

Between 1680 and 1775 white emigration to North America still contained a significant proportion of unfree labourers, but it was also characterized by a greater number of free migrants and a more heterogeneous mixture of strangers entering the colonies. Recent estimates suggest that 307,400 white emigrants came to the thirteen British colonies in North America in the first three-quarters of the eighteenth century. Some 151,600 (49.3 per cent) were free migrants. A further 52,200 (17 per cent) were transported convicts. The remaining 103,600 (33.7 per cent) consisted of indentured servants. These people were much more ethnically diverse than seventeenth-century settlers coming to America, who were overwhelmingly of English stock. The composition of emigrants to America by geographical background for the period 1700–75 was as follows: 35.3 per cent were Irish, 27.4 per cent were German, 23.8 per cent were English or Welsh, 11.5 per cent were Scots, and the remainder came from elsewhere. The Scots were the only group that did not contribute a significant portion of the unfree migrants: almost three-quarters of emigrants from Scotland were free settlers. The free emigrants, of whatever background, flowed into all parts of North America from East and West Florida in the South to Nova Scotia in the North. A significant proportion of them sailed from European ports to exactly the same areas as the unfree migrants. This chapter is not specifically concerned with the free emigrants, significant though they were, because the focus of this study lies with slaves and indentured servants in British North America before 1800. In the analysis below, however, comparisons are made with free migrants where they throw light on the stream of bound labourers.

The potential destinations for these settlers was larger than in the first half of the seventeenth century. Whereas six British colonies had been established on the North American mainland before 1660, twelve were settled by 1700. Georgia joined them in 1732 to complete the thirteen American colonies under British rule before 1776. The number and distribution of the eighteenth-century servant emigrants to these colonies can be briefly summarized. The exact total of English and Welsh indentured servants who relocated in North America is unknown but they numbered about 27,200 between 1700 and 1775. On the eve of the American Revolution, 79 per cent of these servants went to the Chesapeake colonies, the same major destination as in the seventeenth century. Pennsylvania was the next colony favoured by these migrants. Irish emigration to colonial America centred on the Delaware Valley, where there were well-established trade connections between the main Irish ports and Philadelphia. Ships carrying Irish passengers also sailed to Baltimore and New York. From 1730 to 1774 almost 52,000 emigrants left Irish ports for Philadelphia and New Castle, Delaware. They were a mixture of free passengers and indentured servants: probably a fairly even split between the two types of migrant, though the sources for investigating this matter precisely are imperfect. They came to America in peaks and troughs, with the late 1720s and the decade after 1763 witnessing fairly extensive Irish migration to America.

German migration to America was heavily focused on Philadelphia. Some 80,969 German-speaking immigrants passed through that port between 1683 and 1775. This comprised 73 per cent of the flow of German migrants to America in that period. Pennsylvania was a lure for Germans for several reasons. William Penn had established his colony as a haven of religious toleration for people of all races and creeds. Germans had settled in Germantown, on the outskirts of Philadelphia, as early as 1683. And the province, with its extensive rolling farm country, had a reputation from the early eighteenth century as the 'best poor man's country', somewhere where hard work could tap material abundance to achieve good living standards. German settlers in colonial America were partly free passengers and partly 'redemptioners': a form of servitude explained below. The trade ebbed and flowed over time. The peak period was between 1749 and 1754, when 37,000 people from the Rhine lands and satellite territories entered the Delaware River.

Between 1718 and 1775 some 50,000 convicts were shipped to the American colonies from the British Isles. The traffic only came to an end with the coming of the War of Independence. Of the total shipped across the Atlantic, at least 36,000 were from England, more than 13,000 from Ireland, and a mere 700 from Scotland. Unlike the trades in redemptioners or indentured servants, the annual flow of convicts was more regular. One would expect this situation given that transported felons were enforced migrants put aboard ship as British gaols were emptied. Virtually all of the convicts ended up in Virginia and Maryland, though the British government did not compel contractors to send them there. The Chesapeake was a suitable destination for exiled British convicts because they could be dispatched on ships in the tobacco trade and were useful workers in diversifying economy of late colonial Virginia and Maryland.

Similarities and Differences between Convicts, Redemptioners and Indentured Servants

The differences between the three main groups of unfree white workers that peopled the eighteenth-century American colonies need to be established so that one does not confuse them. From previous sections of the book dealing with the seventeenth century, indentured servitude is the most familiar of these institutions. The way in which such servants arrived in the colonies was similar in the eighteenth century to what had occurred before. In other words, people seeking a new life in America but unable to afford their passage signed a written contract or indenture before leaving the Old World. In Ireland such agreements were made before the mayor of the port of embarkation. It fell to him to ensure that the contract had been entered into voluntarily and that minors were only shipped via this method with the consent of their parents or guardians. The indenture was a binding legal document that specified the length of service. Such servants had their Atlantic crossing paid by ship captains. Their labour could be leased in America to masters for a set number of years.

Indentured servitude had some features in common with convict transportation and the redemptioner system that will be discussed below, but it nevertheless remained a distinct and distinctive form of bound labour. It also had some differences as a labour institution to its fore-runner in the Chesapeake before 1680. In the eighteenth century, the practice of some servants arriving at their American destination without a written indenture and then being subject to the 'custom of the country' was less in evidence. The length of the contract was usually four years maximum rather than anything from four to seven years. Freedom dues were less common as part of the contract, or not offered at all. Some colonies continued to provide land for servants who had served their terms. In the early years after the founding of Pennsylvania the proprietor William Penn desired that servants should be given fifty acres of land at an annual quitrent of two shillings. (A quitrent was rent in money or kind in lieu of services.) Penn also wanted the masters given fifty acres at four shillings' rental per annum. But he discontinued this practice around 1700. The early influx of indentured servants to Georgia in the 1730s received between twenty and fifty acres of land when their contract expired, plus cattle, working tools and a cash allowance.

The redemptioner system was almost entirely confined to German-speaking people. Prospective migrants unable to pay their fare to cross the ocean from their European port of departure, frequently Rotterdam, signed a contract in German in which they agreed to redeem their fare after arrival in America. They then usually worked for the person who had redeemed their fare for a certain number of years, their contract specifying that they were 'passengers', 'redemptioners' or 'freight' to be assigned. They paid fixed costs for the Atlantic crossing but could negotiate the length and terms of their service. Various ways of settling the debt were possible. Sometimes redemptioners called on family and friends in Pennsylvania to assist them, drawing on networks of people who might share the same Pietist denomination or who came from their home territory in the German-speaking lands. Alternatively, they settled their fare when they stepped off ship in Philadelphia by paying the captain with money or goods they had brought with them. On other occasions they took out short-term credit, in the form of bonds or promissory notes, to guarantee to redeem their passage fare. Redemptioners, unlike indentured servants, did not enter their contract until disembarkation. The labour part of their contract did not come into effect until their freight money was paid.

In these ways, the redemptioner system, which only began in the 1720s, was more flexible than indentured servant migration. This is particularly the case with the chief characteristic of the contract signed: the right to vary the length of time specified in the agreement in accordance with the size of the debt owed. In the early eighteenth century, passengers were allowed several weeks or sometimes months to settle their fares; but by the early 1770s there was a maximum time of two weeks. Those who crossed the Atlantic by this method were sold as indentured servants in Pennsylvania if they could not raise the money in time. This happened more frequently in the peak period of German immigration to America in the 1750s than before. Accordingly, a good many redemptioners found themselves working for masters who had taken out a contract for their labour for a period of years. In the early 1770s a hybrid contract known as the 'indenture of redemption' appeared in Pennsylvania. Farley Grubb has explained how this operated: 'The immigrant signed an indenture at embarkation but this indenture could be 'cancelled' (as opposed to 'assigned') at the immigrant's discretion at debarkation, and the immigrant allowed to proceed like a redemptioner. This contract gave the immigrant the pre-voyage insurance of a fixed-indenture contract but also the post-bargaining flexibility of the redemption contract.'[1]

The characteristics of the convict trade were somewhat different. Dr Johnson exaggerated when he called Americans 'a race of convicts',[2] but his remark highlighted the significant proportion of transported felons in the population of British North America in the late colonial period. Convicts accounted for about a quarter of all British immigrants arriving in North America in the first three-quarters of the eighteenth century. Though they had been shipped from the Restoration period onwards on a voluntary and relatively small basis, the system of dispatching them to the colonies changed decisively in 1718. In that year Parliament passed a Transportation Act (4 Geo. I, c. II) in an attempt to rid Britain of the crime wave that hit London after the end of the War of Spanish Succession in 1713. The new Hanoverian regime felt that one way to preserve social stability was to banish many offenders sentenced in quarter sessions and assize courts at a time when neither imprisonment nor provision of hard labour at home were considered stern enough punishments. For the first time, courts had the statutory authority to banish felons from the realm; and the 1718 Act ensured that colonial complaints and laws attempting to prohibit the importation of felons would be disallowed by the Privy Council.

The exile of convicts served British rather than American needs. There was no imperial design with regard to penal transportation before 1775: a situation that contrasts with the more active role of the state in the early years of Botany Bay as a dumping ground for felons after 1787. Occasional suggestions were made that convicts could be used to supply hemp or flax for the navy, or that their work could strengthen communities in the American colonies. But these proposals for the more effective use of convict labour did not lead to the setting up of any public-works programmes in North America. Moreover, during the era of 'Salutary Neglect' when the Duke of Newcastle was foreign secretary, there were neither sufficient British officials in North America nor the will to promote schemes that would rehabilitate convicts once they had served their sentences. The chief aim of the 1718 Act always remained banishment.

Characteristics of Bound Servants

The characteristics of eighteenth-century English indentured servants can be reconstructed from registration lists for London covering the periods 1718–59 and 1773–5. The first document stemmed from a parliamentary Act of 1717 designed to prevent the kidnapping of minors and to gain the consent of servants that they should be bound to the colonies. The contracts had to be signed before the Lord Mayor of London. The later list arose from a Treasury order to record all emigrants leaving the country at a time when the British government was worried about possible depopulation. Both sources have been investigated thoroughly by David Galenson in *White Servitude in Colonial America*. The Treasury list has been analyzed exhaustively in Bernard Bailyn's *Voyagers to the West*. For the relatively limited number of English indentured servants included in these lists, there is fuller information on their sex distribution, age structure, occupational skills and geographical background than can be found for either the Irish indentured servants or the German redemptioners.

The two lists provide details on 6,896 servants, of whom only 524 (7.6 per cent) were women. This represents a proportional decline of a half in the number of female indentured servants compared with the equivalent seventeenth-century migrants. This may have reflected supply conditions. A possible explanation is that sufficient work was generated in the late pre-industrial English economy for women, particularly in relation to boosting family incomes, and that this reduced their propensity to emigrate. On the demand side, a greater balance between the sexes existed in North America in the eighteenth century, compared with the founding generations of the colonies, leading to a reduction in the shortage of wives and of females relative to males. Most servants were in their late teens and early twenties: at least two-thirds of the people recorded in the lists were aged between fifteen and twenty-five. Details on the regional origins of the indentured servants enumerated in the London list for 1718–59 show that England provided 98 per cent of the migrants and Wales only 2 per cent. This cohort of English indentured servants came from all over the country but predominantly from the metropolis and its environs. London and the Home Counties accounted for 47 per cent of the servants migrating from 1718 to 1729, 53 per cent from 1730 to 1739, and 39 per cent from 1749 to 1759. By contrast with seventeenth-century English indentured servants, those who migrated to America after 1700 were more skilled. Some 57 per cent of the men registered in London between 1718 and 1759 had skills; by 1773–5 the proportion had risen to 85 per cent. Many of these skills were in non-agricultural occupations. This reflected the growing manufacturing base of the English economy, both in towns and countryside; but it also echoed North American demand for skilled labour in the construction trades and in the metal and wood crafts. By the mid-eighteenth century, importers of servants were making specific requests for skilled workers. Thus the Philadelphia merchant house Willing & Morris noted in the 1750s that 'men and youths ... Good husbandmen, house carpenters, weavers, joyners, smiths, hatters, masons ... and laborers are the best trades.'[3] Most skilled servants, it seems, left England not so much because they were in desperate straits, though some probably had been under-employed at times, but because they were attracted by the lure of America, where the standard of living among most of the white population was at least the equal of that in Britain on the eve of the American Revolution.

Lack of registration lists for Irish emigrants over a significant period of years makes it difficult to disentangle the proportion of free passengers from those coming to America under indenture. However, around two-thirds of the Irish arriving in the Delaware Valley between 1730 and 1763, when total Irish immigration to America was moderate, were probably indentured servants. In the decade after 1763 the situation was different. At that time Irish immigration was at its highest level to North America before the American Revolution. More than 40 per cent of the immigrants from Northern Ireland – which supplied a larger flow of passengers than Southern Ireland – came as fare-paying emigrants in family groups. That so many were able to afford their transatlantic passage reflects the general economic expansion found in Ireland in those years. They were joined in America by a significant number of fare-paying free emigrants from Yorkshire, Scotland and London coming in family groups in the 1760s and early 1770s, some leaving their homes as a result of high rents, the interference of tyrannical landlords and economic distress, others attracted by the magnet of America as a destination where betterment beckoned.

Irish indentured servants were drawn from all over Ireland; there was no single area that provided a large outflow, though numerically most came from Ulster. They were from mixed religious backgrounds. About a quarter of Irish emigrants to eighteenth-century North America were Roman Catholics – the most prominent branch of Christianity in the emerald isle – but Presbyterians, Quakers and Anglicans could also be found among the immigrants. Insufficient material exists to determine whether shiploads of Irish servants were homogeneous groups. The reasons for migration were highly varied. L. M. Cullen has characterized the impetus behind this diaspora as a complex mixture of dynamism, persecution and poverty.[4] At certain times, notably during the Irish famines of 1729 and 1740–1, subsistence problems were a significant 'push' factor. Even so, those particular migrations resulted from complex triggers. 'The reasons those unhappy people give for their going are as various as their circumstances,' a contemporary observed in 1729. He continued: 'Their ignorance leads them' and the 'poorer sort are deluded by the accounts they have of the great wages given there [in America] to laboring men'.[5] Religious intolerance and economic and political discrimination, especially the British penal laws against Catholics, also played their part in decisions to emigrate.

Redemptioners were drawn primarily from the Rhine lands, the Protestant Swiss cantons and other German-speaking areas of western and central Europe. They migrated for complex reasons, including the desire to avoid economic instability, political upheaval and religious persecution in their homelands. They sometimes fled military service, compulsory labour in German principalities, or an oppressive tax regime. Although radical Pietists – Mennonites, Schwenkfelders, and so on – are often cited as characteristic German migrants, they in fact only contributed about 5 per cent of the German settlers in the American colonies. German-speaking people leaving Europe for America were, in addition, a secondary migration. Far more of their compatriots fled their homes for eastern European areas such as Prussia, the Habsburg Empire and Russia than ever sailed across the Atlantic. In contrast with the indentured servants and convicts who came to America, many Germans travelled in family groups. Kin relationships beyond immediate nuclear families were also significant features of these emigrants. Marianne S. Wokeck's authoritative work indicates that between one-third and one-half of these people sailed on ships with relatives among the other passengers.[6] The age distribution of these migrants varied over time. Generally, however, there were more redemptioners in their early and mid-twenties than those who were older. In the 1750s, during the peak period of German immigration to America, a higher proportion of young, single, unattached migrants sailed across the Atlantic, a reflection of the pressures that 'pushed' them out of their homelands. Investigation of the geographical origins of these people is hampered, unfortunately, by lack of good statistical data.

British convicts, as one might expect, had different characteristics to the German migrants. They were sentenced by the courts as either capital offenders or non-capital felons. The former were exiled for fourteen years or life after receiving pardons from the death penalty. The latter – by far the majority – were given seven-year sentences. Most had been convicted of grand larceny, defined as theft of goods worth more than a shilling, not including thefts worth more than four shillings from shops or those exceeding thirty-nine shillings from homes. The crimes that came under the heading of grand larceny included stealing furniture, articles of clothing, food and jewellery. Between 1718 and 1775, some 54.1 per cent of the English convicts were sentenced in London, Middlesex and the Home Counties; the rest came from all over England and Wales, the next highest catchment area being the Western Assize circuit (with 12.8 per cent). Around 80 per cent of the convicts were male; most were between fifteen and twenty-nine years old; nearly all were drawn from the lower orders; and most had committed crime through economic necessity.

Recruitment and Shipment

The redemptioner trade was mainly organized on a triangular axis between three ports: London, Rotterdam and Philadelphia. Three-quarters of the German immigrants took boats up the Rhine to Rotterdam. They had to stop at many toll stations on the way. London shippers provided vessels and liaised with merchants in the Dutch port to freight the ships via Britain, to comply with the Navigation Acts, en route to Philadelphia. Various means of recruiting redemptioners took place. Newlanders, those who had returned to the Rhine lands after a successful trip to America, acted vigorously as recruiting agents. Letters from relatives who had already relocated to America were influential in persuading people to emigrate. Promotional literature proliferated in Switzerland and the German states extolling the advantages of settlement in America. German-language newspapers carried reports from Pennsylvania. Several promotional books became best sellers, notably Gottlieb Mittelberger's *Journey to Pennsylvania* (1756), published just after the peak of German migration to eighteenth-century America.

The indentured servant trade from the British Isles to America involved easier arrangements for shippers. English indentured servants were placed aboard cargo vessels leaving London, Bristol and Liverpool in a similar way to the seventeenth-century practice. Most migrants who ended up in the Chesapeake colonies were accommodated on ships primarily used for the tobacco trade. Irish servants sailed on vessels already used to the shipping lanes from Dublin, Cork, Belfast and Londonderry to Philadelphia. These ships took linen and provisions on their outward journeys and returned with cargoes of flaxseed for the Irish linen industry. Irish merchants publicized their voyages among agents operating in and around the main Irish ports. These recruiting networks appear to have been particularly effective in Ulster. Merchants also placed elaborate advertisements in Irish newspapers, sometimes with signed letters from grateful passengers who had already made the Atlantic crossing. There was nothing equivalent to the German newlanders. Thus, although letters from friends and kin in America doubtless stimulated some Irish men and women to emigrate, organized return visits by those who had made a success of their American sojourn were uncommon.

There was a flourishing trade in English convicts mainly organized by a few London merchant firms who received a Treasury allowance for conducting such business. This amounted to £3 per head in 1718 and to £5 per head from 1727 until the subsidy ended in 1772. The only English provincial port that shipped convicts in large numbers was Bristol, where contractors received fees from various towns and counties for dispatching felons. Most Irish convicts came from the province of Leinster and the trade was mainly conducted through Dublin. Contracting merchants had to take all the convicts they received from gaols regardless of sex, age, health or skill; but they could sell them on arrival in America and pocket the profits. Convicts were placed in irons and shackles and accommodated on ships designed for carrying freight; the places where the felons were stowed beneath deck were usually filled with tobacco hogsheads for the return journey from Virginia and Maryland.

The ocean crossing was often rigorous for whatever type of passengers. Several contemporary descriptions recount the sufferings on board ship experienced by bound migrants to America. Mittelberger's *Journey to Pennsylvania* is perhaps the most graphic of these accounts. He noted cases of German emigrants being cheated out of money and possessions by unscrupulous merchants, captains and newlanders. He also stressed the discomfort of the Atlantic voyage: 'During the journey the ship is full of pitiful signs of distress – smells, fumes, horrors, vomiting, various kinds of sea sickness, fever, dysentery, headaches, heat, constipation, boils, scurvy, cancer, mouth rot.'[7] He continued in this vein at some length. Though one suspects that some of his details were flights of fancy rather than a reflection of reality, for many passengers the ocean crossing was the most momentous voyage they ever took: they were uprooting themselves from their social milieu and most never returned. Contemporary evidence suggests that conditions on Irish emigrant ships were probably less crowded and stressful – and voyages certainly shorter – than on vessels carrying German redemptioners. Felons had an especially bad transit. They were chained and huddled in cramped quarters aboard ship; they received barely sufficient provisions; and they frequently suffered from typhus (known as 'gaol fever') and other diseases picked up in the dirty environment of English and Irish prisons. Nevertheless mortality rates fell from about 14 per cent per voyage in the 1720s to beneath 5 per cent by the 1770s. The mortality rate on voyages carrying Germans was lower. Between 1727 and 1805 it was 3.8 per cent for vessels bringing these immigrants to Philadelphia.

The Criminality of Convicts

One issue that affected the character of the transported felons, but not most of the other bound emigrants discussed in this chapter, was the matter of criminality. Roger Ekirch argued in *Bound for America* – the best recent book on felons transported to North America – that convicts were 'reasonably serious malefactors' who composed 'Britain's most dangerous citizenry.' These judgements are supported by several contentions: that grand larcenists often stole goods worth substantial sums of money; that transported felons included many multiple offenders; and that 'among returning felons, members of British gangs were amply represented'.[8] This portrayal of convicts as serious criminals is nevertheless counterbalanced by another argument, in which the author insists that the same people were not primarily responsible for crime in the Chesapeake. He cites court records for Kent County, Maryland and the Northern Neck of Virginia for the 1730s and 1740s to argue that very few convicts were prosecuted for felonies or misdemeanours in the Chesapeake, and that most criminal acts were carried out by more respectable segments of the community. Lack of convict involvement in crime, Ekirch suggests, was not the result of better economic opportunities in America: it was due, rather, to less scope for theft in the Chesapeake than in Britain – something partly attributable to a greater dispersal of population outside of an urban setting.[9]

These arguments can all be challenged. To insist that convicts were serious criminals when they sailed from Britain but were not much involved in crime during their American sojourn seems contradictory unless one believes that some transformation of their character, social environment, or economic conditions occurred. It seems to me that both arguments may be inaccurate: the one statement exaggerating the proportion of serious offenders who left Britain as transported felons, the other underestimating their criminal activities in the Chesapeake. It may be that transportees were often multiple offenders, though what proportion fell into this category has not been established for virtually any district of England and Wales. But it is questionable whether most grand larcenists were serious criminals and whether convicts returning to Britain commonly resumed membership in gangs. Grand larcenists usually received seven-year sentences for small-scale theft such as stealing single items of household goods or small sums of money. Such crimes were usually carried out opportunistically; they were the result of destitution rather than a criminal disposition. And John Beattie's research has established beyond reasonable doubt that most criminal gangs in eighteenth-century England were not long-lasting and had neither a permanent organization nor a fixed membership.[10]

Moreover, the suggestion that convicts were not significant perpetrators of crime in America needs more supporting evidence before it can be accepted: more evidence from court records in the Chesapeake is needed showing that crime was regularly detected and brought before the courts in Virginia and Maryland. One needs also to explain whether the many American comments insisting that convicts were purveyors of crime were based on fact or were manifestations of paranoia. The anxiety felt in Virginia about transported felons lies behind Governor Robert Dinwiddie's advice to George Washington, then leader of a

Virginia militia regiment, to enlist servants in the Seven Years War but not convicts because the felons 'probably may be fractious, & bad Examples to the others'.[11] It can also be seen in the comment of a Virginia contractor for selling transported felons, who noted that 'people are afraid of convicts as waiting men'.[12] Benjamin Franklin made the most famous of the negative remarks about convicts when he stated that rattlesnakes would be a suitable return to the mother country for dumping felons in the colonies, and that 'the emptying their jails into our settlements is an insult and contempt . . . and would not be equal'd even by emptying their jakes [i.e. chamber pots] on our tables'.[13]

Work and Treatment

There appear to have been changes in the Chesapeake in the perception of convicts' criminality over time. Alan Atkinson has suggested that convicts were treated similarly to indentured servants between 1718 and the early 1740s; in that period they usually undertook seven-year periods of service, whatever their sentence in Britain, and could claim freedom dues on completing their term. These convict 'rights' were determined by local custom that considered perpetual bondage an inappropriate state for Christians. But Atkinson has also argued that from the 1740s until 1775 convicts were treated more as criminals, stigmatized more than indentured servants, and cut off from common rights and freedom dues in Virginia and Maryland. His conclusion is that this change over time in the treatment of convicts stemmed from an increasing concern in the Chesapeake with the moral basis of citizenry.[14] The evidence to support these contentions is stronger for Virginia than for Maryland. The Virginia Assembly passed an Act of 1748 prohibiting convicts from giving evidence in law courts. A later Virginia Act of 1753 deprived convicts of freedom dues. There may have been significant differences between Virginia and Maryland, however, in stigmatizing convicts: the evidence suggests that Maryland treated transported felons as convicts and not as indentured servants from the years immediately after the 1718 Act.

Why were convicts so readily put to work in the colonies despite strong misgivings about their character? The economic answer lies in the supply of slaves, indentured servants and convicts to the Chesapeake colonies before the American Revolution. For most of the eighteenth century there was a perfectly elastic supply of slaves to the Chesapeake. These arrivals and the burgeoning population of American-born blacks were now often trained by planters for skilled agricultural work. Economic diversification in the Chesapeake during the mid-eighteenth century nevertheless created a need for skilled labour for non-plantation work. Since the prices paid for slaves were high in this region and blacks were normally trained for fieldwork on plantations, the solution to this problem seemed to be the importation of white indentured servants. But an inelastic supply of skilled servants, in part the result of rising wages and improving economic opportunities in England in the early eighteenth century, meant that the demand could be met only sporadically. The need for labour for non-plantation work in the late colonial Chesapeake could therefore be met on a regular basis only by cheap convict labourers. Convicts were probably also bought by smaller planters and tradesmen lacking the wherewithal to purchase slaves.

In looking at the role of convicts in the Chesapeake labour market, one must decide whether convict work was interchangeable with that of bonded servants. Bailyn has argued that the distinction between convicts and indentured servants virtually disappeared where labour needs were great in the Chesapeake.[15] Certainly, there were some similarities between convicts and indentured servants in that region in the late colonial period. Convicts were frequently regarded by American purchasers as another form of indentured labour. Both types of workers were dominated by young men in their twenties. Convicts and indentured servants worked in agriculture, industry and the craft and construction trades; both tended to serve similar terms (even though some convicts officially had longer sentences); both seeped out of the dependent labour force at the end of their period of bondage; both were required by law to carry passes when travelling more than a few miles away from their owners' homes; and both ran away frequently, as newspaper advertisements testify. Because of these similarities, some contemporaries thought convicts and indentured servants were stigmatized together because of their lower-class status and dependency. According to William Eddis, an Englishman living in Maryland in the early 1770s, this was because all servants were regarded as outcasts and 'the difference is merely nominal between the indented servant and the convicted felon', a situation which meant that indentured servants were 'indiscriminately blended with the most profligate and abandoned of mankind'.[16]

Yet there were also important differences between convicts and indentured servants. Both forms of labour were cheaper than buying slaves, but skilled convicts were more expensive than indentured servants (if one divides their sale price by their usual term of service). Convict and servant prices fluctuated with commodity prices – notably for tobacco – but by the 1770s a male indentured servant with four years' service sold in Maryland for £9 on average and a female servant for £8. Prices fetched for convicts at the same time in Maryland were £8–9 for women, £10 for men, and £15–25 for skilled men. The prices paid for convicts in late colonial Maryland were affected by purchasers' calculation of the labour value of their criminality. Indentured servants were more skilled than convicts: around 85 per cent of the indentured servants arriving in Maryland in the period 1773–5 – for which full records survive – had a named occupation, whereas runaway advertisements for convicts in the *Maryland Gazette* in the thirty years after 1745 indicate that only 43 per cent of convicts had skills. Further differences were that penal passengers had no freedom of choice about their destination in America or their labour arrangements; and that most convicts, because of the stigma attached to them, tended to abscond with other felons for the most part. Perhaps the greatest difference between indentured servants and convicts was that the latter were increasingly treated as commodities in the Chesapeake labour market. At convict sales in Virginia felons were sold 'in the same manner as horses or cows in our market or fair'.[17] In Maryland transportees were chained together in pairs, driven 'in lots like oxen or sheep', and inspected by prospective buyers who searched them 'as the dealers in horses do those animals in this country' by looking at their teeth and viewing their limbs 'to see if they are sound and fit for their labour'.[18] Branded as outcasts, with little stake in the Chesapeake community, transported convicts found it difficult to prosper in America once they had served their terms. They frequently returned to Britain before finishing their term of service despite the dire penalty awaiting them if apprehended.

Master–Servant Relations

In common with master–servant relations in the seventeenth century, court records reveal the rights of both parties and the tensions that arose between them. As Richard B. Morris has succinctly remarked, the courts considered 'articles of indenture bilateral agreements capable of enforcement by either party'.[19] Certainly, masters and mistresses had a strong legal hold over their servant charges. Servants were still regarded as the chattel property of their employers during the term of their service; their unexpired terms could be bequeathed in wills. Masters held an inherent interest in the property of servants that entitled them to legal redress if a third party interfered with a servant's term of service. In many colonies legislation was passed against those attempting to entice servants away. For example, New York enacted a law in 1684 that stipulated a fine of £5 current money for people aiding and abetting the flight of any servant, and specified further that those found guilty would be charged with the costs and damages incurred by the master. Different legal regulations were laid down for those harbouring servants in colonies such as Pennsylvania, Delaware, New Jersey, Maryland and Virginia. Penalties were stipulated in each instance.

The laws governing runaway servants also protected masters' rights. In New York and New Jersey, under laws of 1684 and 1714 respectively, servant runaways could be sentenced by two justices of the peace. If caught, the fugitives had to recompense the costs and charges of their masters and serve double time to compensate for their absence. In 1683 Pennsylvania legislated that runaway servants should serve an extra five days for each day they were at large. Statutory double extra time was also the practice in Virginia and North Carolina, under laws passed in 1643 and 1715. Maryland had the most draconian legislation of this type. The Maryland fugitive-servant law of 1661 specified an extra ten days' service for each day that a servant absconded. In many of the above instances capture costs would be taken into account by courts and converted into additional days' service for fugitives. Beyond punishments for runaway servants, the general codes that dealt with indentured servants included a range of punishments for disobedience. These regulations were especially strict in the tobacco colonies; they included corporal punishment, occasionally imprisonment, and even more occasionally the death penalty for capital crimes.

The legal treatment of servants was not entirely biased towards masters, however, for those under indenture had certain legal rights. As in the seventeenth century, servants had full testimonial capacity in court; they could also bring witnesses into the courtroom to corroborate their charges. Servants had the right to petition courts with their complaints. This was the main way in which they sought redress of grievances. These rights served to check many cases of maltreatment by masters, who were required to provide decent food, shelter and clothing for servants during their term of service. Many court cases document instances where servants' rights were infringed. To take one example, in 1692 John Walter petitioned Henrico court, Virginia, on behalf of fellow servants. These people had been treated stingily, 'their victuals being So ill dressed that they Could not Eat it, and their bed So short, and the Cloathing soe mean that they could not keep themselves warm with it'.[20] The result of the appeal is unknown.

The sale of servants, a widespread practice in eighteenth-century America, was checked in Pennsylvania under a statute of 1700. This forbade masters and mistresses from selling servants in another colony without the consent of a justice of the peace. It also limited the sale of servants within the province by specifying that at least one justice had to be present to ensure fair play. Legal records show that servants were frequently successful at law in the Chesapeake when they sought relief because of poor food, inadequate shelter and ragged clothing provided by masters. And in every case prior to 1774 in the Court of General Sessions of New York County, servants who brought cases alleging bad conduct against their masters were successful. In several colonies local courts freed servants from their uncompleted time when masters were found guilty of misdemeanours. This occurred in New York as a result of legislation passed in 1684; it was also the normal practice in eighteenth-century Pennsylvania and New Jersey.

The Experience of Servitude

The above account suggests that the masters' rights over servants were considerable but also that well-defined legal means of redress were available to indentured labourers. It is not always possible to find out whether the various laws relating to servants were enforced fully or partially, but the scholarly literature on the subject indicates that enforcement usually occurred after decisions had been taken in court. For the eighteenth century, there is more material to draw on than for the seventeenth century to ascertain how servants were treated. Examples of the abuse of servants abound. One can find instances of masters hitting and beating servants for not signing their indentures properly and feeding them only with bread and water. Eddis considered 'generally speaking' that in Maryland c. 1770 indentured servants 'groan beneath a worse than Egyptian bondage'.[21] Poor clothing and a grimy appearance could bring to surface images associated with servants and their status. Franklin, in his *Autobiography*, recalled an incident in 1723 when he spent the night at a poor inn in New Jersey, where, with his wet clothes and dishevelled appearance, he 'made so miserable a figure' and was 'suspected to be some runaway indentured servant'.[22] Many similar contemporary complaints could be supplied. Some modern historians have concurred that the servants' lot was a poor one in the colonies. Representative of this view is Gordon S. Wood's comment that 'in the colonies servitude was a much harsher, more brutal, and more humiliating status than it was in England'.[23]

Scattered bits of surviving correspondence by indentured servants seem to support this gloomy verdict. William Moraley, who took out an indenture for five years in 1729, considered, on the basis of his experience in New Jersey, that 'the condition of bought Servants is very hard'. When servants appeared in court to charge masters with non-performance of their duties, Moraley noted that 'the Master is generally heard before the Servant, and it is ten to one if he does not get his Licks for his Pains'.[24] Elizabeth Sprigs, who arrived as an indentured servant in Maryland in the 1750s, wrote back to her father, 'What we unfortunat English people suffer here is beyond the propibility of you in England to conceive, let it suffice that I one of the unhappy number, am toiling almost Day and Night.'[25] Baikia Harvey, a sixteen-year-old indentured servant who arrived in Georgia from Scotland in late 1775, wishes she had taken her grandfather's advice to stay at home. 'I beg that none of my Relation[s] may come to this Country,' she wrote him, 'Except they are able to pay their passage thir selves and then they may come as soon as they like this is a good poor mans Country when a man once getts into a way of Liveing but our Country people knows nothing when they come hear.'[26]

A more hopeful assessment came from a Scottish storekeeper in Prince George's County, Maryland, a few years before the War of Independence, when a fresh influx of servants entered the colonies. He drew a distinction between older and younger indentured servants. 'As to themselves, especially when in advanced years,' he wrote, 'the change of climate, hardships they often undergo during their Servitude, under tyrannical masters, with the pressure on their minds on being rank'd & deemed as Slaves, are such, that they seldom surmount – As to the younger Class, it is otherwise, for they become more easily habituated to the Clime, are better able to undergo any hardships, & their servitude for a few years, is in my opinion of service to them & may be looked on only as an apprenticeship, in which they become acquainted with the names, customs of the country, Culture of its different produce.'[27]

The authentic voice of the indentured labourers illumines the institution in which they served much more vividly than for their seventeenth-century counterparts, where similar correspondence is almost entirely lacking. How representative were these generally pessimistic responses to servitude? Modern research provides arguments and data that can be marshalled for both positive and negative assessments. The most detailed attempt to examine whether indentured servants were poorly treated in eighteenth-century North America focuses on Pennsylvania. In the only modern book-length consideration of servitude as an institution in the British American colonies, Sharon V. Salinger has argued that the treatment of servants changed over time in that province. Between the founding of Pennsylvania and the 1720s, when most immigrants came from England, she considers that servitude was a benign, paternalistic, largely rural institution based on oral agreements, personal ties and minimal overt conflict between masters and employees. From the 1720s to the mid-century, however, she suggests that the system altered. German and Scotch-Irish servants now outnumbered those from England. Indentured servitude became more impersonal, exploitative, harsh and urban, with most servants clustered in Philadelphia. The institution became dominated by written contracts. In this scenario, relations between servants and masters became more brutal and led to a higher incidence of servants running away. The position of servants deteriorated further in the quarter century before the War of Independence, especially after 1763, when labour surplus replaced labour scarcity in Philadelphia, wage rates fell below the cost of unfree labour, a decreasing amount of capital was available for investment in servants, and a vacillating economy required more flexible work arrangements. The transition from unfree to free labour brought changing contractual relationships between masters and employees. Such shifting labour relations brought struggles and insecurity to the servant class.[28]

These interesting arguments, unfortunately, are not proven. The suggested transition of servitude in eighteenth-century Pennsylvania from a non-market institution characterized by paternalism to a harsh, impersonal, market institution is not sustained by the evidence marshalled by Salinger. Depiction of servitude as an increasingly urban phenomenon in Pennsylvania founders on the statement that 'in 1745, more than 58 per cent of the servants were bound to Philadelphians, and in 1772, 38 per cent of the servants were purchased by city residents'.[29] The percentage drop cited here for the middle of the eighteenth century demonstrates the reverse of the author's point. In fact, only 24 per cent of the immigrant servants listed in records for Pennsylvania dating from 1746 were bought by Philadelphians. The notion that relations between servants and masters became more brutal and led to a higher incidence of running away remains unsubstantiated. There are instances of both these features of servitude in Pennsylvania, illustrated in many news-paper advertisements for the province, but how representative they were of the totality of the servant experience is impossible to prove. The fact that only 6 per cent of Philadelphia's servants took to their heels by the late colonial period undercuts the notion that increased social conflict occurred between owners and servants.

Nor is it possible to state, without qualification, that the redemptioner system was oppressive. It could be harsh in instances where family members were separated from one another and where newcomers were pressurized to sign indentures on unsatisfactory terms. But it could also be a positive step in one's life cycle. As Wokeck explains, some German immigrants 'accepted this system of temporary servitude either as an educational opportunity or as a rite of initiation into the New World, or they welcomed it as a means to finance an otherwise unaffordable relocation'.[30] German migrants succeeded in creating cohesive ethnic communities in colonial America, making effective use of family net-works, in a way that was not really possible for the indentured servant or convict migrants. Moreover, as Grubb has noted, redemptioners, besides gaining similar compensation to free wage labourers, had certain advantages over their poor, free fellows: they were entitled to food, shelter and clothing all year round, and they could bargain over their contracts on the basis of their skills.[31] Whether this means, on the whole, that servant prospects were good is another matter. To demon-strate that one would need to trace servants after their brief spell as bound labourers, and to investigate their mobility and experiences after they became free. Considerable evidence suggests that labour mobility was common in the American revolutionary era, and it is likely that many servants ended up going westwards to the frontier. What hap-pened to them there is largely unknown. The difficulties of carrying out such research are presumably the reason why even such a detailed study of late colonial servitude as *Voyagers to the West* did not trace the fate of servants after their terms expired. Until historians provide such studies for Pennsylvania, Virginia and Maryland, we will not be able to assess the opportunities for ex-servants systematically.

Notes

1. Farley Grubb, 'Labor, Markets, and Opportunity: Indentured Servitude in Early America, a Rejoinder to Salinger', *Labor History*, 39 (1998), p. 237 n. 14.
2. James Boswell, *The Life of Samuel Johnson*, ed. G. B. Hill, rev. and enlarged by L. F. Powell, 2 vols (Oxford, 1934; orig. pub. 1791), ii, p. 312.
3. Historical Society of Pennsylvania, Philadelphia, Thomas Willing to John Perks, [?] Oct. 1754, Willing & Morris letterbook (1754–61).
4. L. M. Cullen, 'The Irish Diaspora of the Seventeenth and Eighteenth Centuries' in Nicholas Canny (ed.), *Europeans on the Move: Studies on European Migration, 1500–1800* (Oxford: Clarendon Press, 1994), p. 114.
5. Public Record Office of Northern Ireland, Belfast, Ezekiel Stewart to Michael Ward, 25 Mar. 1729 [Educational facsimile no. 122: Emigration].
6. Marianne S. Wokeck, *Trade in Strangers: The Beginnings of Mass Migration to North America* (University Park, PA: Pennsylvania State University Press, 1999), p. 51.
7. Oscar Handlin (ed.), Gottlieb Mittelberger, *Journey to Pennsylvania, 1756*, trans. John Clive (Cambridge, MA: Harvard University Press, 1960), p. 12.
8. A. Roger Ekirch, *Bound for America: The Transportation of British Convicts to the Colonies, 1718–1775* (Oxford: Oxford University Press, 1987), pp. 4, 5, 29, 55–6, 210.
9. Ibid., pp. 167–93.
10. J. M. Beattie, *Crime and the Courts in England, 1660–1800* (Princeton: Princeton University Press, 1986), pp. 256–7.
11. Robert Dinwiddie to George Washington, 19 Aug. 1756, in W. W. Abbot et al. (eds), *The Papers of George Washington*, Colonial series, 3 (Charlottesville, VA: University Press of Virginia, 1984), p. 359.
12. Alderman Library, University of Virginia, Harry Piper to Dixon & Littledale, 24 Oct. 1767, Harry Piper letterbook.
13. Franklin to the printers of the [Pennsylvania] *Gazette*, 9 May 1751, and Franklin to the printer of the *London Chronicle*, 9 May 1759, in Leonard W. Labaree et al. (eds), *The Papers of Benjamin Franklin* (New Haven, CT: Yale University Press, 1959–), iv, pp. 131–3, viii, p. 351.
14. Alan Atkinson, 'The Free-Born Englishman Transported: Convict Rights as a Measure of Eighteenth-Century Empire,' *Past and Present*, no. 144 (1994), pp. 88–115.
15. Bernard Bailyn, *Voyagers to the West: Emigration from Britain to America on the Eve of Revolution* (New York: A. A. Knopf, 1986), pp. 260, 264, 324–5.
16. Aubrey C. Land (ed.), William Eddis, *Letters from America* (Cambridge, MA: Harvard University Press, 1969), pp. 37–8, 40.
17. William Barker, Jr to John Palmer, 16 Dec. 1758, as quoted in Frederick Hall Schmidt, 'British Convict Servant Labor in Colonial Virginia' (College of William and Mary Ph.D. dissertation, 1976), p. 156.
18. William Green, *The Sufferings of William Green* (London, 1774), p. 6.
19. Richard B. Morris, *Government and Labor in Early America* (New York: Columbia University Press, 1946), p. 502.

20. Virginia State Library, Richmond, Henrico Court Order Book, v, fo. 285.
21. Land (ed.), William Eddis, *Letters from America*, p. 38.
22. Kenneth Silverman (ed.), Benjamin Franklin, *Autobiography and other Writings* (Harmondsworth: Penguin Books, 1986), p. 25.
23. Gordon S. Wood, *The Radicalism of the American Revolution* (New York: A. A. Knopf, 1992), p. 53. A similar comment appears on p. 54.
24. Susan E. Klepp and Billy G. Smith (eds), *The Infortunate: The Voyage and Adventures of William Moraley, an Indentured Servant* (University Park, PA: Pennsylvania State University Press, 1992), p. 96; the phrase from the quotation 'get his licks' could be rendered as 'get a whipping'.
25. Elizabeth Sprigs to John Sprigs, 22 September 1756, quoted in Isabel M. Calder (ed.), *Colonial Captivities, Marches and Journeys* (New York: National Society of the Colonial Dames of America, 1935), pp. 151–2.
26. Baikia Harvey to Thomas Baikie, 30 Dec. 1775, in Barbara De Wolfe (ed.), *Discoveries of America: Personal Accounts of British Emigrants to North America during the Revolutionary Era* (Cambridge: Cambridge University Press, 1997), p. 211.
27. John Campbell to William Sinclair, 26 July 1772, ibid., p. 156.
28. Sharon V. Salinger, *"To Serve Well and Faithfully": Labor and Indentured Servants in Pennsylvania, 1682–1800* (New York: Cambridge University Press, 1987).
29. Ibid., p. 174.
30. Wokeck, *Trade in Strangers*, p. 158.
31. Farley Grubb, 'The Auction of Redemptioner Servants, Philadelphia, 1771–1804: An Economic Analysis', *Journal of Economic History*, 48 (1988), pp. 586–92; Grubb, 'Labor, Markets, and Opportunity', p. 239.

CHAPTER 4

Slavery in the Eighteenth Century

The eighteenth-century witnessed the heyday of the British slave trade and a rapid upsurge in the number of enslaved Africans in North America and the Caribbean. During that period vessels fitted out primarily in Liverpool, London, Bristol and Newport, Rhode Island – the one major slaving port in North America – exported around three million slaves from west Africa. These captives were taken from six main areas: Senegambia, Sierra Leone, the Gold Coast, the Bight of Benin, the Bight of Biafra and west-central Africa. The proportion taken from each area varied over time owing to complex patterns of supply and demand, but overall far more slaves were taken from the Bight of Biafra to British America than from any other African region. Most of these slaves ended up in the Caribbean rather than on the American mainland. For instance, in the 1720s only 24,000 (15.8 per cent) out of an estimated total of 152,000 slaves arriving in British America came to the mainland colonies. In the period 1766–75 a similar situation prevailed. Some 36,800 Africans (13.1 per cent) of the 279,000 that came to British American territories entered the southern mainland colonies. The much larger proportion of slave arrivals in the Caribbean reflected the back-breaking work, wide range of diseases, and high mortality rate among black workers in that region and the consequent need to replenish the black population regularly through new imports. The smaller number of slaves taken to North America resulted from a more uneven distribution of regional slave labour than in the West Indies, lesser demands in the Chesapeake for a large plantation workforce, and the emergence of a significant number of creole (i.e. American-born) slaves because of a better demographic situation.

Slave labour was found in all the British North American colonies from Maine to South Carolina in the late seventeenth century, but it was more important in some than others. Broadly speaking, the proportion of African-Americans in a colony's population increased as one moved from north to south, with most slaves clustered south of the Mason-Dixon line. In 1750, for instance, 210,400 (86.9 per cent) of the 242,100 slaves in North America lived in the Chesapeake and Lower South. Table 4.1 presents the estimated size of the black population in different American regions in the eighteenth century. Less than 3 per cent of the New England population and less than 8 per cent of the Middle Colonies' population was black. On the other hand, by 1740 African-Americans comprised 28 per cent of the Upper South's population and 46 per cent of the Lower South's. By 1780 the black share of the Chesapeake population had increased to 39 per cent, while the African-American element in the Carolinas and Georgia had slightly declined to 41 per cent. From 1710 until c. 1755 South Carolina was the only British North American colony with a black majority; thereafter Georgia also exhibited this pattern.

These figures nevertheless conceal variations within regions. There were parts of individual colonies where slavery was more significant than in the colony as a whole. In New England more slaves were found in Rhode Island than in any other colony. This was connected to Newport's role in the slave trade and to the mixed economy of the Narragansett region around Newport and Providence: blacks were sometimes brought back via the West Indies on Rhode Island slaving vessels and employed in stock farming and dairying. A Rhode Island census of 1774 indicated that 14 per cent of households in the colony

Table 4.1 Estimated black population in British North America, 1700–80 (in thousands)

Year	New England	Middle Colonies	Chesapeake	Lower South	Total
1700	1.7	3.7	12.9	2.9	21.2
1710	2.6	6.2	22.4	6.6	37.8
1720	4.0	10.8	30.6	14.8	60.2
1730	6.1	11.7	53.2	26.0	97.0
1740	8.5	16.5	84.0	50.2	159.2
1750	11.0	20.7	150.6	59.8	242.1
1760	12.7	29.0	189.6	94.5	325.8
1770	15.4	34.9	251.4	155.4	457.1
1780	14.4	42.4	303.6	208.8	569.2

Source: John J. McCusker and Russell R. Menard, *The Economy of British America, 1607–1789* (Chapel Hill: University of North Carolina Press, 1985), pp. 103, 136, 172, 203.

owned slaves. In the Middle Colonies, slaves were mainly clustered in the Hudson River valley, in parts of eastern New Jersey and in the two port cities of Philadelphia and New York, where they were employed in agriculture, at ironworks, in urban trades, and in households as domestic servants. By the 1750s about 70 per cent of the wealthier craftsmen in the Quaker city owned slaves. In prosperous areas of the Chesapeake, where growing tobacco cultivation was productive, more than half the population had slaves by the 1760s. In South Carolina, the black majority was particularly evident in some rural areas in the rice-dominated Lowcountry where blacks could outnumber whites by two to one.

Variations in the incidence of slavery suggest that 'the peculiar institution' had a distinctive impact on different areas of North America in the eighteenth century. Following a distinction referred to in Chapter 2, most parts of the northern colonies were slaveowning societies while the southern colonies were slave societies. The work, culture and treatment of slaves varied partly on the basis of this concentration of numbers of blacks in a colony, town, county or parish. Ira Berlin has recently reiterated this point but he locates it more within a temporal perspective. His interpretation suggests that the seventeenth-century black experience was a 'charter generation' in North America, characterized by the emergence of Atlantic creole communities, where blacks worked reasonably harmoniously alongside whites and were not subjected to degradation. This was followed in the first three-quarters of the eighteenth century by the 'plantation generation' where racial lines hardened as the staple economies absorbed ever more numbers of enslaved blacks. After 1775 came the 'revolutionary generation' in which slavery and the growth of free black communities took divergent paths in various North American regions.[1] This chapter outlines the shifting spatial and temporal perspectives of slavery in the eighteenth-century colonies, with particular emphasis on the impact made by the plantation on slaves' lives.

Demography on the Plantations

The demographic composition of the slave population shaped the parameters of slave life in North America. Sex ratios, age structure and the relative proportion of African and creole slaves influenced reproductive rates, family formation and black culture. Though the relative proportion of males and females in the Atlantic slave trade varied over time and by region, generally there was a demographic imbalance in the trade. Males outnumbered females, often by a ratio of two-to-one, partly because women were prized in Africa as workers. North American colonies that depended heavily on an influx of new slaves from Africa therefore tended to import more adult men than women. Apart from the unbalanced sex ratio, several other factors affected the reproductive capacity of Africans taken to America. Of the adult female slaves, a significant proportion were already advanced in terms of childbearing years. African women invariably practised prolonged lactation of up to three years, which acted as a natural contraceptive. The epidemiological shock experienced by people entering a new continent and new disease environment tended to produce above average mortality rates. These factors meant that fertility among newly-arrived African slaves in America tended to be low and mortality relatively high. This naturally created severe problems for family formation. Colonies where creole slaves predominated produced a more balanced sex ratio because the share of boys and girls born would be more equal (at any rate, certainly not two-to-one in favour of males). In addition, births occurred at an earlier stage of a woman's life cycle, adaptation to a new disease environment was not a problem, and consequently fertility increased while mortality waned.

Exceptions occurred to these generalizations but they still explain why most North American slaves in 1700 were imported Africans but most slaves in 1776 were creoles. At the outbreak of the American War of Independence only 20 per cent of the slaves in the thirteen colonies were African-born. But there were significant differences in the plantation colonies between the demographic experience of the black population in the Chesapeake and the Lowcountry. The chief contrast lay in the more rapid rise of a native-born slave population in the Upper South. This was a process well under way by the second quarter of the eighteenth century. It became an even more notable feature of Chesapeake society in the generation before the Revolution. In the Lower South the proportion of black creoles in the population also rose during the eighteenth century but more slowly. The slave trade continued to South Carolina up until 1808, when Thomas Jefferson's government finally stopped it, whereas slave importations into Virginia and Maryland had effectively stopped in the late 1760s and early 1770s.

The black population in Virginia and Maryland was heavily dependent on an African influx between 1690 and 1740. Africans were imported to all the major river systems of the western shore of the Chesapeake Bay where tobacco planting flourished. Thereafter rapid population growth among slave families enabled planters to cut back on freshly imported slaves as the black population experienced sustained natural growth. A contemporary clergyman realized that this transformation had begun by the 1720s, for he remarked that 'the Negroes are not only encreased by fresh supplies from Africa and the West India islands; but also are very prolifick among themselves'.[2] In 1728 about half of the adult black slaves had arrived in the Chesapeake colonies within the last decade; by 1750 the proportion was 17 per cent. A third of the enslaved workers in Virginia and Maryland were Africans in the 1750s, by which time the demand for newly imported Africans came mainly from the interior piedmont areas of the region, where tobacco planting was expanding westward to escape soil exhaustion. Two decades later only a tenth of the slave population of the Chesapeake had been born in Africa. This was a remarkable demographic transition within less than a century, for few New World slave populations experienced such good rates of population growth and the rise of a creole-dominated plantation workforce.

In the early eighteenth century several disincentives prevented the early emergence of many creole slaves in the Chesapeake. One in four saltwater slaves died during their first year in Virginia and Maryland, mainly from malaria or respiratory illnesses. Slaves arriving from Africa were sometimes housed in segregated compounds. This, coupled with the scattered nature of slave quarters, the low population density of the black population, and the excess of males over females among adult imported slaves, militated against a demographic upsurge. But as the survivors among the new slaves had children, a better balanced sex ratio developed. Creole slave women proved more fertile than Africans, largely for the same general reasons already mentioned; on average, they bore six children whereas African-born female slaves bore three. Moreover, native-born black women married earlier than African women, often entering wedlock in their late teens. This increased their legitimate childbearing years. Plantation sizes increased in Virginia and Maryland after 1750, and as slave quarters grew in size and black population density followed suit, more opportunities arose for personal liaisons and relationships among male and female slaves. Most slaves in the Chesapeake lived in families by the 1770s and cross-plantation networks among them were common.

South Carolina was heavily dependent on African-born slaves until 1750 or thereabouts. In the first half of the eighteenth century, an excess of males over females characterized the black cargoes entering Charleston, with probably a relatively high proportion of children. Owing to the disease environment of the Lowcountry, childhood mortality rates may have climbed as high as 50 per cent. If so, they probably soared above the usual rates of infant mortality found on West Indian sugar plantations: another demographic killer in the plantation Americas. The hard work of rice cultivation took its toll on adult slaves: a high proportion died while still in their prime. Between 1720 and 1740 Charleston's slave imports reached their highest levels yet, enabling planters in the province to top up their workforce with new arrivals. The aftermath of the Stono Rebellion of 1739 curtailed the arrival of Africans for virtually a decade as South Carolinians, shaken up by a slave revolt led by Africans, decided to cut back on 'new Negroes'. Native-born blacks therefore had the time to reproduce in the 1740s. After 1750, the South Carolina slave population was beginning to reproduce itself. Governor James Glen recognized this demographic growth when he noted that 'importations' of slaves to the colony were 'not to supply the place of Negroes worn out with hard work or lost by Mortality which is the case in our Islands where were it not for an annual accretion they could not keep up their stock, but our number encreases even without such yearly supply'.[3] In fact, this was too sanguine. A surplus of births over deaths was achieved among the South Carolina slave population after 1750 but the reproduction rates were three or four times lower than in the Chesapeake. It is thus unsurprising that South Carolinians continued to take a strong interest in the Anglo-American slave trade until its demise. Native-born blacks in the Palmetto colony comprised 37 per cent of adult slaves in 1730, 44 per cent in 1750, and 56 per cent in 1770.

Slave Work

Productive work for white masters was the chief *raison d'être* for importing and employing enslaved Africans in the New World. Most of the waking hours of slaves, on at least six days of the week, were spent toiling for their owners without any wages. In the North American context, slave work varied over time and according to regional economic demands. In New England and the Middle Colonies there were no staple crops that required a plantation labour force. Moreover, reliance on family labour in many rural households – especially in New England, where good reproduction rates among whites produced sizeable families – meant that recruiting workers from outside the household was a secondary option. Nevertheless, blacks could be found working in a wide range of agricultural and industrial tasks and trades in the northern colonies. In port cities such as New York and Philadelphia, where the reliance on slave labour increased during the first half of the eighteenth century, slaves worked in the maritime trades as sailmakers, coopers and dock workers; they often assisted artisans and tradesmen in shops and workshops; and female slaves found a niche as domestic servants. Middling craftsmen and artisans in New York and Philadelphia increasingly employed one or two slaves after 1750, finding them a useful source of labour when indentured servants were unavailable or wage labourers proved too costly to hire.

Slaves also worked in the rural agriculture of the northern colonies in the eighteenth century. Northern farmers were increasingly replacing servants with slaves in colonies such as Pennsylvania, New Jersey and New York during the first half of the century. They mainly held slaves in ones or twos. In the Narragansett Bay area of Rhode Island, as previously noted, slaves could be found in larger numbers, with some stock-rearing farms employing up to twenty slaves. The other extensive rural form of employment for slaves in the northern colonies consisted of ironworks, situated especially in New Jersey and Pennsylvania. Some of these forges employed between thirty and fifty slaves to work alongside white indentured and free workers. As John Bezís-Selfa has shown, the deployment of African-Americans at ironworks helped entrepreneurs gain control of the pace and costs of charcoal iron production, which required a large number of seasonal tasks throughout a yearly cycle. It also enabled owners to discipline white workers by placing them in a worse bargaining position for their labour because of the presence and availability of slaves as an alternative workforce.[4]

Two chief characteristics of slave work in the northern colonies were that African-Americans' labour was regarded as interchangeable with that of various free and unfree white workers, and that work was carried out by individuals or in small groups working together. Supervisory arrangements, as a result, tended to be flexible, especially where blacks were working in masters' households. The situation in the southern colonies was fundamentally different: though domestic slaves were employed and some blacks were assigned artisan tasks, the majority of slaves toiled on plantations producing staple crops for export. The work regimes on plantations were partly determined by the much greater agglomeration of blacks within a limited space; but they were equally shaped by the particular seasonal demands of staple crops. This can be illustrated by consideration of the different rhythms and organization of slave work on Chesapeake tobacco estates and on rice plantations in South Carolina and Georgia.

Slaves working on tobacco plantations were subject to long hours of work. A contemporary observer, William Tatham, noted that they laboured 'from daylight until the dusk of the evening, and some part of the night, by moon or candlelight, during the winter'.[5] Work filled up six days of the week. Holidays were usually restricted to just three days a year: Christmas day plus one day each at Easter and Whitsun. Midday lunch breaks were pared back to the minimum time needed to bolt down food. Cultivating tobacco was nowhere near as backbreaking for slaves as sugar cultivation, but it involved regular, monotonous work over a seasonal cycle that lasted from the beginning of the year until the autumn. Slaves prepared land for planting tobacco in January or February. The seed was sown in February and March in newly cleared mulch beds. April saw extensive hoeing and weeding. The ground needed to be tilled regularly until August, when the tobacco harvest began. Slaves cut the tobacco leaves, let them lie in fields for half a day, and then took the leaves to a tobacco house, where they hung them. They stripped the leaves from the stalk before rolling the tobacco and prizing it into hogsheads. These activities required close supervision; any slackness or mistreatment of the tobacco leaves could ruin a planter's annual crop.

Gang labour characterized most of the work done on Chesapeake tobacco plantations in this seasonal crop cycle. Under this system, slaves worked in units of commonly nine to twelve workers. Their pace of work was determined by the leader of the gang, a black foreman, under the watchful eye of a white overseer; sometimes the managers of plantations also turned up in the tobacco fields to oversee the work routines. Since managers and overseers tended to place fit, young, male slaves in the position of foreman, the pace of the work – at its most intense during the hoeing and weeding during the spring – could exhaust other members of the gang, who were required to work in lines and keep up with the foreman. Thus a certain amount of regimentation occurred (though not as much as in the larger gangs on Caribbean sugar estates). Individuals were closely monitored. Disagreements frequently occurred between the overseers and the gang labourers. The patriarchal tobacco planter Landon Carter typified the attitude of owners to their gangs when he once threatened a foreman at his Sabine Hall estate with 'a sound correction' unless he 'mended his pace'.[6] Men, women and children all laboured in the tobacco fields. Women, in fact, comprised a higher proportion of field workers tending this crop than men as the eighteenth century progressed; and boys and girls were usually working in the fields by the age of nine.

Gang labour maximized productivity for planters. There was little relief for black workers because tobacco required constant attention and the leaf could mature at any time in August or September. Long hours of work gave slaves only limited opportunities to cultivate their own provisions or to engage, like their West Indian counterparts, in huckstering or private subsistence activities. In their spare time on Sundays slaves usually confined any manual labour to tending their own garden plots within the estate. The hard work of slaves on tobacco plantations was exacerbated by two factors. Tobacco was a crop that regularly exhausted the soil. Usually it could not be grown productively on the same land for more than three years in a row. The need to clear new land added to the work burdens of slaves. And since tobacco exhausted the soil, planters started to acquire land away from the original tidewater settlements and expand into the interior of the Virginia and Maryland, setting up new plantations in the hilly, piedmont country beyond the fall lines of the great Chesapeake river systems. By the mid-eighteenth century slave work on tobacco estates was intensified by this process because, in addition to cultivating new land, much of the piedmont area was heavily forested and slaves had to clear the woods, hoe the land and plant fresh crops rapidly.

The general pattern of slave work on the Lowcountry rice plantations followed a different pattern. The seasonal cycle was longer, lasting from twelve to fourteen months, and the work much more arduous and unhealthy. Tough manual labour characterized most stages of the production process. It was carried out in swampy areas inhabited by insects, reptiles and mosquitoes. Disease and physical danger were part and parcel of rice cultivation. As Alexander Hewatt observed in 1779, 'no work can be imagined more pernicious to health than for men to stand in water mid-leg high, and often above it, planting and weeding rice'.[7] There was no equivalent to the rigours of rice production among the staple economies of North America, for tobacco, as explained above, was not so difficult a crop to cultivate. The nearest equivalent to rice cultivation in British America was sugar production in the Caribbean, which took a similar toll on energy and health.

The cycle of rice production began in January and February when slaves cleared land and trees with axes. The rice was sown between April and June. Workers pressed seed into waterlogged ground, often using their heels to cover the plant with mud. Over the summer fields were flooded to encourage the seed to sprout. After the rice began to germinate, fields were hoed to eliminate weeds and a process of alternate flooding and draining of fields was necessary to provide sufficient moisture for the rice to grow. Substantial irrigation works were often needed to reclaim river swamp. Slaves exerted great effort in constructing dams, building embankments, clearing ditches, and constructing canalized links between rivers and swamps. Often slaves were standing knee-deep in swamp and mud to carry out these tasks. Middleburg estate, a notable Lowcountry rice plantation, contained more than fifty-five miles of bank covering six million cubic feet of earth. If one were to calculate the amount of earth included in all the rice plantations in colonial South Carolina and Georgia, they would rank as one of the largest hand-built earthworks to be found anywhere in the world.

In August, during the peak heat and intense humidity of summer, black workers had to ward off birds from raiding rice in the fields, a task carried out with guns. The rice harvest began in mid-September and a further sequence of complex tasks followed: stacking the rice into large ricks, threshing and winnowing; pounding the rice to remove the grain's outer husk and inner film; storing the rice in warehouses. As winter approached, many post-harvest tasks were combined with preparing land for the next season's planting. Virtually all of these tasks were carried out by hand, though some threshing machinery had appeared in South Carolina by the 1760s and 1770s. Though the tasks varied at different stages of the production cycle, they were nearly all potentially exhausting and, because of the disease environment, sometimes debilitating. Rice itself, when harvested, was abrasive to the hand. One of the most unpleasant manual tasks consisted of pounding the rice with mortars and pestles – a tiring process that could take hours and leave aching muscles and sore palms. The demanding nature of pounding by hand was relieved somewhat in the generation before the American Revolution with the introduction on some estates of pounding machines driven by livestock.

Rice plantations covered a large acreage. They usually had more slaves attached to them than Chesapeake tobacco plantations. By 1750 a third of South Carolina's slaves lived on plantations with more than fifty black labourers; some rice estates had a slave force in excess of 100 people. Rice was a more straightforward crop to grow than tobacco; it did not require the same degree of close supervisory attention during the production cycle. For this reason, plus the expanse of many rice plantations, the normal method of work on South Carolina and Georgia estates consisted of task work supervised by either a white overseer or a black foreman, known as a driver, or both. Unlike Chesapeake tobacco plantations, where owners tended to live year-round in a Big House within the estate's grounds, planters in the Lower South often spent part of the year as urban grandees in towns such as Charleston and Savannah, leaving supervision on the spot to the overseers and drivers. Task work was followed at each stage of rice production. The basic unit in the fields in the mid-eighteenth century was a quarter of an acre per day. But tasking was also used for pounding (measured by the number of mortars used) and for fencing (measured by the number of poles put up) and for other aspects of work. As in the Chesapeake, the field labour force was disproportionately made up of women, though adults of both sexes and children often worked together at different stages of the seasonal cycle.

Rice therefore, like tobacco, was a lucrative staple commodity that had work patterns associated partly with the nature of the crop. For slaves, task work had several benefits. They could carry out their allocated daily portion of work at their own pace. Industrious workers could hope to complete their tasks by early afternoon. Slaves were supervised less directly, allowing them to become self-reliant at work and able to adapt their work practices without too much direct interference. Planters were careful not to impinge on the slaves' time off work or the day of rest on the Sabbath. In the extra time they had as a result of efficient tasking, blacks could devote more time and attention to cultivating their own grounds, which were larger than those in Virginia and Maryland. They grew potatoes, pumpkins, melons, peanuts and corn. They kept some fowl. The produce arising could be marketed in an internal economy. In these ways, slaves in the Lower South accumulated cash and exercised a fair degree of autonomy over their lives. But the world of tasking in the Lowcountry was hardly a rosy affair. Disputes frequently arose between slaves and their white superiors over the time needed to complete certain tasks. Often these disagreements were based on slaves insisting they had worked hard and worked sufficiently on a given day and overseers challenging their output. For instance, in 1774 three slaves owned by George Austin absconded in early December 'for being chastis'd on Account of not finishing the Task of Thrashing in due time'.[8] This reminds us of the recourse to slaves running away in South Carolina and the whippings and beatings of slaves that occurred frequently.

Master–Slave Relations

The repression involved in relations between masters and slaves led some contemporaries to take a gloomy view of the pattern of control and obedience that lay at the core of chattel slavery. 'The whole commerce between master and slave', wrote Thomas Jefferson, was 'a perpetual exercise of the most boisterous passions, the most unremitting despotism on the one part, and degrading submissions on the other.'[9] Certainly, the legislation on slavery enacted by colonial legislatures after 1660 and the range of punishments that whites could mete out to blacks appear to support this sombre view of master–slave relations. Virginia's first major slave code was passed in 1680 and strengthened in 1705. South Carolina had a series of slave codes, including detailed legislation enacted in 1712 that was tightened up in 1740 after the Stono Rebellion had alarmed the Lowcountry planter class. A statutory law of race and slavery existed in all thirteen British North American colonies by the middle of the eighteenth century. These acts singled out slaves as a caste. On paper they were draconian, allowing for a wide range of physical punishments including branding on the cheek or thumbs, amputation of body limbs, splitting noses, castration, and the death penalty, each one applied according to the nature of wrongdoing by slaves. Under these laws, slaves lacked various rights: the right to marry, the right to testify in court, the right to challenge the hereditary nature of slavery. Examples abound of how these vehicles of white dominance were inflicted on slaves.

Despite powerful instruments of coercion and compulsion, however, master–slave relations were not as unremittingly bleak or as harsh as the above paragraph suggests. One major reason why this was so lay in the spread of patriarchy as the main ideological underpinning of slave control during the eighteenth century. Large planters in the Chesapeake, men such as the Carters of Nomini Hall or the Tayloes of Mount

Airy, were imbued with the spirit of patriarchy. A similar situation can be found with the grandee planters of the Lowcountry, such as Henry Laurens. Patriarchy meant acting towards slaves as a father figure, recognizing that black workers were part, as it were, of an extended household. William Byrd of Westover, Virginia, realized that he played this role. 'Like one of the Patriarchs,' he wrote to the Earl of Orrery, 'I have my Flocks and my Herds, my Bond-men and Bond-women, and every soart of Trade amongst my own Servants, so that I live in a kind of Independence of everyone but Providence. However this soart of life is attended without expense, yet it is attended with a great deal of trouble. I must take care to keep all my people to their Duty, to see all the Springs in motion and make everyone draw his equal Share to carry the Machine forward.'[10] Byrd recognized, as this statement shows, that the role of a patriarch could be difficult.

While a patriarch could act in a stern, cold, distant way, he could take great interest in the everyday lives of slaves and ensure that African-Americans could conduct their own family lives on plantations with a reasonable amount of autonomy. Good work and behaviour by slaves would be rewarded by patriarchs with gifts and possibly promotion to skilled tasks or positions in the master's household. But opposition, recalcitrance, absconding would bring down on the slave the punishments that a dutiful father felt was appropriate to control his charges. During the eighteenth century, patriarchy on the American plantations modulated into paternalism. This was a complex process, not occurring everywhere at a similar time, but visible by the latter part of the century. The shift from patriarchy to paternalism – a process continued in the antebellum era – was influenced by Enlightenment concerns for benevolence towards others and progress in human society, by a greater number of creoles in the slave population who did not have to be broken into slavery, and by a gradual change in attitudes in western society about inflicting bodily pain. Patriarchal attitudes emphasized order, obedience, hierarchy and subjection; they displayed few illusions about the potential rebelliousness of slaves. Paternalistic attitudes, on the other hand, proffered a generous treatment of slaves and expected gratitude in return; they promoted the myth of the happy, contented bonded black worker.

George Washington is a prominent example of a planter whose treatment of slaves reflected this change. His views about his Mount Vernon estate and his black workers were a mixture of commercial, patriarchal and paternalist attitudes. Sometimes one of these three models dominated his behaviour as a planter, but it would be simplistic to separate them into distinct modes of thought; they intermingled to make up a complex view of slavery. Washington took a commercial view of slavery as a business, wanting to make profits from tobacco and grain cultivation, oversee agricultural improvements, and keep debts to a minimum. This outlook underscored the fact that the Mount Vernon slaves were also his chattel. He also had patriarchal attitudes that he had absorbed from the planter culture of his youth in Virginia. These manifested themselves in strict control of slaves after the manner of a father figure looking after dependants; they meant he acted distantly and sometimes rigorously towards his slaves. But paternalistic elements also existed in his mind: these were reflected mainly in his concern for slave families and their personal relationships and in his dislike of splitting up slaves who had established such ties. The beneficent side of Washington's treatment of slaves is depicted in Junius Brutus Stearns' painting *Washington as a Farmer at Mount Vernon*, which shows him paternally overseeing his slaves and his stepgrandchildren. Washington realized his control of African-Americans required mutual obligations even though he did not identify emotionally with their plight. It is not surprising that each of the three models – commercial, patriarchal, paternalist – underpinned Washington's personal dealings with slaves, for all appear to have been in a state of redefinition in North America in the late eighteenth century.

Slave Society and Culture

Given the lack of much direct testimony from the slaves themselves, modern archaeological research, combined sometimes with architectural reconstruction, has provided an insight into the material standards and quality of life experienced by blacks in the eighteenth-century American south. In recent years, such investigations have proliferated. They have been linked with work in museums, where many artefacts found on plantations can be checked and identified against existing samples. Comprising an important aspect of the re-creation of the past for modern visitors to sites associated with slavery, they enable the material realities of slave life to be understood in a way that is often not possible from written documents because plantation day books and account books tend not to include such facets of ordinary slave life and work. They also project the living conditions of slaves to a much wider public than historians, and in so doing help to shape public consciousness of the legacy of slavery.

In the Lower South, perhaps the most fruitful excavations have been undertaken at Middleburg estate, a former rice plantation situated on the Cooper River near Charleston. The slave houses there either rotted or were torn down in the nineteenth century. But since the site has not been worked over and does not suffer from soil erosion, fragments from artefacts and investigation of soil colours around the foundation level of the eighteenth-century slave quarters have been excavated by archaeologists under the leadership of Leland Ferguson.[11] At Middleburg plantation the slave quarters were erected with mud walls and thatched roofs. They closely resemble huts built in Africa but are laid out according to the European desire for a symmetrical formation of buildings. Substantial evidence of pottery manufacture has been established for the plantation, with designs that emanated from west Africa. The pottery includes cooking jars and eating bowls. Other artefacts gleaned from the Middleburg site indicate that slaves actively hunted and gathered their own food beyond the rations allocated to them that are sometimes mentioned in plantation records. Fragments of turtle bone have been found in a rubble pile. Bones excavated indicate that Africans on the estate ate a varied diet, including chicken, pork, beef, deer, catfish, quail and possum. Samples of bones from other South Carolina plantations show that slaves also ate frogs, squirrels and raccoons. Fish hooks, fish weights and gun flints have been found, indicating that slaves were fishing the creeks and rivers that run through the plantation and using guns to hunt.

Equivalent archaeological investigations have taken place in recent years at various plantation sites in Virginia. Many of these are on-going, and it may be that the most interesting conclusions are yet to appear. The entire buildings and estate at Monticello, Jefferson's mountain-top home near Charlottesville, were designed by Jefferson himself over a forty-year period from 1768; but the house, the gardens and the tobacco farms were all constructed by slaves. Archaeological reconstruction of the slave quarters at Monticello has been aided by a precise plan made by Jefferson in 1796, in which he described every building and gave it a letter. These buildings were situated on Mulberry Row, which originally contained nineteen houses in a 200-yard strip that also included utilitarian structures containing examples of light industry and fenced-in gardens between each building. Work on the slave dwellings with the letters [R], [S] and [T] has proceeded on sites where a number of artefacts have been found. They include examples of English pearl ware, which was an expensive form of ceramics; enough tea cups and other tea-ware to form a tea set; decorative-style wine glasses; gaming pieces such as dominoes; fragments from musical instruments, notably a fiddle bow; a slate with words engraved on it; and fragments from pencils. These artefacts point to a richer slave culture than we would find in written documents. Doubtless some of them were acquired from white personnel at Monticello.

Lest we should think that the material life of slaves was cosy, the dimensions and bare furnishings of slave quarters should be remembered. Slaves usually lived in small, spartan log cabins about twelve feet by fourteen feet. The spaces between the logs were filled with mud. Only one original eighteenth-century slave house survives in the Old Dominion, a building from southern Virginia, so attempts to reconstruct slave dwellings from before the Revolution are based on quite slender architectural evidence. Such a reconstruction, however, is under way at Carter's Grove plantation, on the outskirts of Williamsburg, the former capital of Virginia where half the eighteenth-century population consisted of unfree black workers. This reconstruction is being carried out using eighteenth-century methods and tools, so that it will appear as authentic as possible. At Williamsburg such architectural archaeology has been combined with the reconstruction of other houses that originally had eighteenth-century façades and with craftsmen in period costume and tour guides to emphasize not so much the oppressive nature of much slave work but the contribution of slaves to their own survival and the artefacts and dwellings associated with them.

Slave quarters, whether on or off plantations, were near to their place of work. Despite their modest appearance, they usually enabled African-Americans to exercise control over their own domestic arrangements without too much interference from white overseers or managers. Slave quarters afforded little privacy because they were huddled together and often arranged around a communal yard. But they were the site of much of the community and cultural life of slaves. Most Africans arrived alone off shipboard after the end of the Middle Passage. They had been torn from their roots in Africa, often leaving complex family and kinship ties behind them. They entered the Americas as heterogeneous groups with varied ethnic origins. In North America for most of the seventeenth century, when the imbalance in sex ratios saw too many men and too few women, the construction of slave families was not easy. But with the growth of a creole slave population in the eighteenth century slave families became more common, notably in the Chesapeake colonies, where, as explained above, fertility among black women was high. Slave children were taken by their mothers to the fields on plantations while their mothers toiled away at manual labour. They were looked after by their mothers until about the age of ten, often helping out with work on estates from the age of six. Between the ages of ten and fourteen most slave children left the parental home to live with brothers, sisters and relatives. By the late eighteenth century, a rich set of family networks was common in North America as African-Americans used the base of family obligations, love and affection to sustain their spirits and wellbeing.

Slave customs and cultural beliefs testify to a rich blend of African practices and adjustments to life on a new continent. They provided a focal point for black communities. Slaves enjoyed music and dance, playing a wide range of musical instruments ranging from fiddles to horns and percussion. They sang at work to ease the boredom and rigours of the labouring routine. In 1774 Nicholas Cresswell, a British visitor to Maryland, described how on Sundays the blacks 'generally meet together and amuse themselves with Dancing to the Banjo'. He added that 'their poetry is like the music – Rude and uncultivated. Their Dancing is most violent exercise, but so irregular and grotesque.'[12] Slaves told folk stories often linked with memories handed down from African traditions. In their limited leisure time, these facets of musical and oral culture came to the fore, frequently involving entire slave communities. They were accompanied by festivals and parades at Christmas, the New Year, Easter and after the crop harvest. Spiritual values were an essential part of slave communities. A belief in spirits often seemed mere superstition to white observers; but it was bound up with a commonly held black belief that spirits cast spells that could harm or cure, something that was linked to medicinal treatments for ailments by the use of herbs. Though African beliefs that filtered through to America had many variations, they all acknowledged the existence of a supreme being and they all invoked the spirits of nature and ancestors. Life's major staging posts – birth, marriage, death – were all steeped in spiritual significance for slaves. Funerals, in particular, were observed with a high degree of ritual and ceremony because many blacks believed that death marked a return to Africa.

Efforts to Christianize North American slaves were carried out from the beginning of the eighteenth century. The Society for the Propagation of the Gospel in Foreign Parts (the SPG), with headquarters in London, was particularly energetic in proselytizing the Christian message. Active especially in South Carolina, the SPG nevertheless found it difficult to convert more than a handful of slaves. They disapproved of slaves working on Sundays on their garden plots, which affronted their sense of Sabbatarianism. They also ran into conflict with slaves who openly failed to behave monogamously in their sexual relationships, considering this sinful in the eyes of God. It was not until the 'Great Awakening' of the 1740s and the religious revivalism that swept parts of the South in the 1750s and 1760s that large numbers of slaves were converted to Christianity. These evangelical stirrings of the soul were associated largely with the Presbyterians, Methodists and Baptists, who favoured itinerancy, extempore preaching, minimizing doctrinal differences, conversion as a result of God's saving grace, open-air gatherings, fervent hymn singing, and the prospect for all who joined the Christian faith and maintained their faith to live in the hope of everlasting peace in the life hereafter. Such evangelical exhortation had a widespread appeal to blacks as well as the ordinary white population. In the 1750s the Presbyterian evangelical preacher Samuel Davies wrote that there were 'multitudes' of Virginia blacks 'who are willing, and even eagerly desirous to be instructed, and to embrace every opportunity for that end'.[13]

Among the preachers who cared about converting slaves to Christianity, no-one was more effective than George Whitefield, the Calvinist Methodist whose preaching took America by storm on seven trips between 1738 and 1770. Unlike John Wesley, who condemned slavery on moral grounds, Whitefield did not attack the institution of slavery, but considered that planters should teach the Gospel to their slaves. Planters sometimes disagreed; there was the uncomfortable realization that baptism of slaves and the evangelical message might steer African-Americans towards the legitimization of freedom. But planter qualms were unable to stem the tide of increasing Christian conversion among slaves in the Chesapeake. By 1776 probably a third of Virginia's Baptists were blacks – testimony to the impact of Protestantism on the slave community at the time of Independence. In the Lower South Christianity spread more slowly among a heavily African-born population that had difficulty in understanding the meaning of preachers' words. Hewatt considered that such slaves were 'as great strangers to Christianity, and as much under the influence of Pagan darkness, idolatry and superstition, as they were at their first arrival from Africa'.[14] The growth of Christianity among the American black population became more pronounced after the War of Independence, however, as African-Americans, especially in the northern states, began to form their own churches and chapels.

The impact of Christianity on American slaves and the growth of paternalism in master–slave relations by the time of the Revolution might lead one to suggest that a merging of white and black culture was in train. One historian, Mechal Sobel, has advocated this view for the Chesapeake, suggesting that a convergence of European and African-American cultures can indeed be found at the time of American independence.[15] This is rather a sanguine view, however, that overemphasizes the coming together of distinct cultures. Christianity had not spread as widely among the whole American black population as the work of Baptists in Virginia implies by 1776, and a flourishing distinct African-American culture was more characteristic of black society than an accommodation between the values of the masters and the slaves. In the Chesapeake after the War of Independence, white attitudes towards slavery hardened, despite the promotion of a diluted anti-slavery message. In the Lowcountry the tightening up of racial attitudes also occurred but without even much of a watered-down attempt at abolitionism. Chapter 6 will explore the ways in which this happened in the wake of the declaration that 'all men are created equal'.

Notes

1. For elaboration of these themes, see Berlin's *Many Thousands Gone: The First Two Centuries of Slavery in North America* (Cambridge, MA: Harvard University Press, 1998).
2. Richard L. Morton (ed.), Hugh Jones, *The Present State of Virginia . . .* [1724] (Chapel Hill: University of North Carolina Press, 1956), p. 75.
3. James Glen to the Board of Trade, 26 Aug. 1754, in Elizabeth Donnan (ed.), *Documents Illustrative of the History of the Slave Trade to America*, 4 vols (Washington, DC: Carnegie Institution of Washington, 1930–5), iv, p. 313.
4. John Bezís-Selfa, 'Slavery and the Disciplining of Free Labor in the Colonial Mid-Atlantic Iron Industry' in Nicholas Canny, Joseph E. Illick, Gary B. Nash and William Pencak (eds), *Empire, Society and Labor: Essays in Honour of Richard S. Dunn, Pennsylvania History*, special supplemental issue, 64 (1997), pp. 270–86.
5. G. Melvin Herndon, *William Tatham and the Culture of Tobacco* (Coral Gables, FL: University of Miami Press, 1969), p. 102.

6. Jack p. Greene (ed.), *The Diary of Colonel Landon Carter of Sabine Hall, 1752–1778*, 2 vols (Charlottesville, VA: University Press of Virginia, 1965), i, p. 430.

7. Alexander Hewatt, *An Historical Account of the Rise and Progress of the Colonies of South Carolina and Georgia*, 2 vols (1779; Spartanburg, SC: repr. The Reprint Co., 1971), i, p. 159.

8. Southern Historical Collection, University of North Carolina, Chapel Hill, Josiah Smith to George Austin, 31 Jan. 1774, Josiah Smith letterbook (1771–84).

9. William Peden (ed.), Thomas Jefferson, *Notes on the State of Virginia* (Chapel Hill: University of North Carolina Press, 1955), pp. 162–3.

10. Quoted in Pierre Marambaud, *William Byrd of Westover, 1674–1744* (Charlottesville, VA: University Press of Virginia, 1971), pp. 146–7.

11. Leland Ferguson, *Uncommon Ground: Archaeology and Early African America, 1650–1800* (Washington, DC: Smithsonian Institution Press, 1992).

12. *The Journal of Nicholas Cresswell 1774–1777* (London: Jonathan Cape, 1925), pp. 18–19.

13. Samuel Davies, *Letters from the Reverend Samuel Davies, Showing the State of Religion in Virginia, Particularly among the Negroes* (London, 1757), p. 10.

14. Hewatt, *An Historical Account*, ii, p. 100.

15. Mechal Sobel, *The World they made Together: Black and White Values in Eighteenth-Century Virginia* (Princeton, NJ: Princeton University Press, 1987).

CHAPTER 5

Slave and Servant Resistance

Resistance to bondage by slaves and servants occurred frequently, as one might expect in a situation where unequal power relationships defined the position of masters and unfree labourers. The form that resistance took varied. For both slaves and servants, unwillingness to perform work adequately, either because their condition engendered negative reactions or because they were badly treated, was a common act of resistance. This could be effected by working below the levels of expected productivity, failing to complete tasks, or sabotaging work routines. In severe cases of disenchantment or alienation from their lot, slaves and servants downed tools and stopped work. Opportunities existed to damage a master's property, to steal food, and to interrupt seasonal work routines. Resistance did not necessarily have a political content; in fact, usually this was not present in acts of defiance. Nor did resistance always have ulterior aims of securing full freedom. Rather, it took the form of negotiation and renegotiation of the parameters of power and compulsion, which, in the case of slaves, had the added dimension of racial polarities. Far from servants and slaves being docile recipients of whatever their masters doled out to them, they determined when and where cooperation should be suspended. This is not to suggest that all slaves and servants, throughout their period of bondage, were actively and continuously impelled by a spirit of opposition to their owners; but it reminds us that, although they left few written statements justifying their actions, we can infer that they reacted to the treatment they received in a robust way.

To oppose white masters was a courageous act, for the penalties could be severe. Fines, whippings, confinement in dungeons, occasional mutilation and removal of privileges are just some of the consequences that met determined acts of resistance. Sometimes brave acts of defiance by slaves and servants had unintended consequences. Malingering by a slave, for example, might lead an owner to the decision that that individual was no longer worth keeping in a plantation gang, possibly leading to the sale of the slave and the break up of black family ties. But though punishments could be severe – and, as the previous chapter has shown, this formed an essential component of patriarchy – masters also dangled the carrot as well as wielding the stick. To deal with acts of resistance it could be more beneficial to allow slaves extra time to cultivate provision grounds or to improve the state of their dwellings, or to give servants extra food and a new suit of clothes, rather than resorting to the lash. In the case of servants, the more draconian punishments were tempered by their right to appear and testify in law courts. In the case of both servants and slaves, masters wanted workers to accede to their owners' wishes.

The most common type of slave resistance was probably flight from a master's purview. This will be examined later in the chapter. The most extreme form of resistance, apart from suicide, took the form of conspiracies and rebellions. These were essentially confined to the slave population; the only revolt in which servants played a significant part was Bacon's Rebellion, analyzed below, and the combined forces of the militia and white governing class in Virginia put this down in such a way that it was unlikely to be repeated. Servants were also not very much involved in rebellions because their bondage was temporary and they seeped out into the free labour force after four years on average. They were then free to marry and to set themselves up independently. Given the heritable nature of slavery, one might expect to find that many slave revolts occurred in North America in the seventeenth and eighteenth centuries. But there were, in fact, more aborted risings than actual revolts; more conspiracy scares than conspiracies that were implemented; and not a single slave revolt that proved successful. Throughout the plantation Americas the only slave rebellion that ever resulted in the overthrow of white power occurred in Saint-Domingue in 1791, where a massive, planned upsurge of 400,000 blacks, led by Toussaint L'Ouverture and inspired by the French Revolution's ideals of liberty, equality and fraternity, saw the overthrow of French overlords and the creation of a black republic. The new regime lasted for over a decade before Napoleon Bonaparte restored French white rule. The Saint-Domingue revolt remained an iconic moment of triumph for all subsequent generations of slaves, and was much feared by statesmen such as Thomas Jefferson, but within the period covered by this book it was only followed by one significant North American slave rising, that by Gabriel Prosser in Virginia in 1800.

Why were slave risings relatively uncommon in British North America between 1600 and 1800? For the first seventy years of this period, the answer is that there were too few slaves for an effective revolt to take place. But the influx of large numbers of Africans to North America in the late seventeenth century coupled with the growth of plantations and the subsequent codification of statutes discriminating against blacks might lead one to expect a more concerted challenge by bonded labourers to their misery. That this did not occur frequently resulted partly from the low density of African-Americans in an extensive terrain until the mid-eighteenth century – Virginia and South Carolina, for example, being much larger geographically than Great Britain. In such circumstances, slaves were accommodated on scattered quarters, which effectively nullified moves to coordinate revolts. The lack of homogeneity among the saltwater slaves plus the residence of slaveowners on their plantations – permanent absentee ownership was rare – contributed respectively to divisions among the black workforce and the constant gaze of white personnel with power. Ironically, the reproductive capacity of the eighteenth-century creole slave workforce, especially in Virginia, and the training of slaves for skilled agricultural work, leading to a pecking order of rewards and responsibilities for the most able workers, might also have served to undercut serious uprisings by ameliorating slave conditions and allowing blacks a meaningful role through which they could gain a measure of autonomy over their lives.

Despite these obstacles to slave uprisings, a number of revolts and conspiracies did occur. Two of these were in New York City. In April 1712 a revolt occurred there in which twenty-five Africans and Indians burned several buildings in Manhattan and killed nine whites. The rising was quelled. Whites exacted their revenge, capturing the rebels and hanging them in chains. In 1741 New York experienced a 'Great Negro Plot'. Surviving documentation is ambivalent on whether this really was a slave conspiracy but it led to thirty blacks and four whites being executed. Its leader Caesar, who had hoped to burn buildings in Manhattan and escape to French Canada, was burned alive. In 1734 an attempt at a slave rising occurred in Somerset County, New Jersey, but this failed. On the eve of the American War of Independence rumours circulated throughout the southern colonies about increasing slave rebelliousness. In the early 1770s attempted slave plots affected Perth Amboy, New Jersey; Ulster County, New York; Norfolk,

Virginia; St Andrews parish, South Carolina; Dorchester County, Maryland; and the Tar River region of North Carolina. Each of these conspiracies alarmed whites but did not cause major disturbances. Each could be looked at further, but in order to understand the distinctiveness of individual slave uprisings and why they failed it is better to analyze three leading events in detail: Bacon's Rebellion in Virginia, the Stono revolt in South Carolina, and Gabriel Prosser's conspiracy in Virginia. Widely separated in time – 1676, 1739 and 1800 – they nonetheless all occurred when white internal divisions were apparent. But they each followed a different course and each ended in failure.

Bacon's Rebellion (1676)

Bacon's Rebellion had a significant impact on the propertied classes in Virginia. Led by a newly arrived planter, Nathaniel Bacon, the rising was an attempt to secure land in the westward part of Virginia by poorer whites who felt deprived of economic opportunity by the wealthy planters of the tidewater, led by Governor William Berkeley. Bacon had been educated at Cambridge University and was sufficiently wealthy to start his life in Virginia by purchasing a tobacco plantation. He was a second cousin of Governor Berkeley. Bacon's motives and his relationship with Berkeley were complex and susceptible of different interpretations. Bacon was initially favoured by Berkeley, being given a place on Virginia's Council soon after settling in the colony. During 1676 Bacon and Berkeley fell out, were briefly reconciled, and then parted their ways again over the matter of dealing with Indians. There had recently been skirmishes between various Indian tribes and white settlers in the Chesapeake over access to land. Blood was spilt on both sides. Bacon, who hated the Indians, repeatedly asked for a commission from Berkeley to attack the Indians with military support. But Berkeley, wanting to trade with the Indians and not wishing to antagonize them, did his best to evade the request. He was worried that Bacon planned to attack Indian tribes indiscriminately rather than to focus a raid on those who had been in conflict with white settlers. On 10 May 1676 Berkeley denounced Bacon and removed him from the Council. But Bacon rounded up supporters to invade Indian lands. They ended up massacring a group of Occaneechees.

Over the summer of 1676 further raids against the Indians turned into a rebellion that was almost a civil war in Virginia. The rising was brief but bloody. Fighting took place between Bacon's supporters and the Indians, leading to casualties. The rebels paraded Indian captives through Jamestown in early September, offering, as they went along, freedom to servants and slaves who would join Bacon. Anyone who offered resistance was attacked. The rebels drove Berkeley out of Jamestown and then torched the town and seized the government for themselves. There was much plunder of property. They devised a political programme and adopted 'Bacon's Laws', which reinstated freemen with the franchise they had lost to freeholders six years before. Not long after this climax to the revolt, Bacon caught a swamp fever and died, probably of dysentery, on 26 October. Without his leadership the rebellion soon petered out. Berkeley, aided by armed vessels arriving from England with a thousand troops, regained control. The rebellion was put down and 'Bacon's Laws' were repealed. Twenty-three of Bacon's supporters were hanged by Berkeley.

This was the largest uprising so far in the history of Britain's colonies in North America. It involved disgruntled ex-servants, other freedmen and slaves joining together to oppose the status quo. About one in ten of the slaves in Virginia joined in the uprising. In 1677 an investigation of the causes of the revolt by the king's commissioners found that a significant part of the rebel force had been 'free men that had but lately crept out of the condition of Servants'.[1] One of the last batches of rebels to surrender consisted of a mixed band of eighty blacks and twenty English servants, who were highly critical of their officers capitulating before they did. T. H. Breen and Edmund S. Morgan, writing independently, have highlighted the fears aroused in Virginia with regard to social and political stability as a result of this unruly amalgam of lower-class rebels joining together over a potential racial divide. They have shown how the aftermath of the rebellion led to moves to tighten slave codes in Virginia and to prize apart any future armed cooperation between slaves and ex-servants. They have also underscored the anxiety that the 'giddy multitude', as contemporaries called them, could wreck the hard efforts of propertied settlers in the Chesapeake and lead to potential anarchy.[2] The problem of social unrest seemed serious to Virginians for the rest of the seventeenth century, especially as new indentured servants continued to arrive in the colony in the 1680s and early 1690s and later found that land was not as readily available as they had supposed when they completed their terms of service.

The Stono Rebellion (1739)

This was the largest slave revolt not just in the history of colonial South Carolina but in the history of the British mainland colonies in North America. It began early on a Sunday morning, 9 September 1739, and consisted of a group of slave rebels breaking into a store near the Stono River in a coastal parish twelve miles south of Charleston. Led by an Angolan called Jemmy, the rebels beheaded two white men, seized weapons and alcohol, and proceeded to march southwards towards Florida. Gathering anything between 50 and 100 recruits along the way, they marched with drums and banners, and destroyed plantation houses and farm houses. By the afternoon they had reached the Edisto River, where they paused in an open field, presumably hoping that extra black recruits would flock to their cause and make them invincible. This gave the white militia time to organize an attack on the rebels, to muster quick support from local planters, and to erect pickets at strategic crossroads and ferry crossings. The rebels and the militia came to blows, and according to a contemporary report 'one fought for Liberty and Life, the other for their Country and every thing that was dear to them'.[3] Some blacks who were not among the rebels supported their planter owners, while others tried to pacify the rebels. By the evening, most of the black resistance had been quelled. However, some slave rebels escaped and the whites who had confronted them in the afternoon skirmish concentrated their efforts on hounding them down. White fears of the rebelliousness stirred up by the uprising were not quelled for a couple of months. Not until the end of November 1739 did a report note that 'the Rebellious Negros are quite stopt from doing any further Mischief, many of them having been put to the most cruel Death'.[4] During the rising at least twenty white people and forty-four blacks died.

The causes of the revolt must remain speculative. Harsh conditions probably played a part. South Carolina had suffered from a bout of epidemic disease in the summer of 1739. The tough work routine of planting rice in swampy Lowcountry areas may have fired some of the resistance. That the Spanish garrison of St Augustine had offered freedom to Carolinian slaves shortly before the uprising broke out was perhaps of greater significance, owing to the proximity of South Carolina to the Spanish border and the fact that the Stono rebels headed south in that direction. Whatever the rebels' motives, we know for certain that this was a rising shaped by African tactics. Most of the rebels, including the leader, were slaves born in Africa rather than creoles. In fact, many of them had been dispatched from Angola and were of Congolese extraction. John K. Thornton and Edward Pearson have shown persuasively that their actions exhibited some notable features of resistance associated with ethnic martial traditions in Africa.[5] For instance, the initial decapitation of the two white men at the start of the revolt mirrored the common resort to displaying severed heads in African societies as trophies of military prowess. The use of banners and drums as the Africans marched south from Stono were integral to fighting methods followed in west-central Africa. It may be that some of the rebels had had experience of war within Africa; this, after all, was how many slaves had been taken as captives before they were shipped across the Atlantic.

The collapse of the Stono revolt was not surprising: there was no unanimity among the blacks involved about its purpose and the afternoon pause near the Edisto River gave the white forces time to organize and counterrattack. But though it seems an exaggeration to view such a short outbreak of black violence as a defining moment in the history of South Carolina and of race relations in North America, it left long-lasting fears among the white minority in the Lowcountry about the potential for similar revolts in the future. Thus the secretary to the trustees of Georgia wrote in his journal that 'the [white] Inhabitants cannot live without perpetually guarding their own Safety, now become so precarious'.[6] The response of South Carolina's politicians to Stono reveals the importance they attached to dealing effectively with the aftermath of the uprising. South Carolina went to war with the Spanish in St Augustine to try to block an obvious avenue of escape for their slaves. The South Carolina Assembly introduced a prohibitive import duty on slaves, which cut back the introduction of African slaves into the province for most of the 1740s. Most important, South Carolina passed a comprehensive slave code in 1740. Drawing on previous statutes, this tightened up the control over slaves and became the basis of the colony's slave law for virtually the next century. The 1740 code laid down larger fines than previously for planters who failed to control their slaves; it took the granting of manumission away from individual planters and placed it under the authority of the legislature; and it included other clauses that led to greater surveillance of black activity in the province.

The Gabriel Prosser Conspiracy (1800)

The Stono Rebellion involved African-born slaves staging an uprising based on African notions of warriorship in a colony where blacks already outnumbered whites. But slave conspiracies and revolts could also occur in situations where creole slaves were the norm and whites were more in evidence. A prominent example of the latter style of uprising occurred near Richmond, Virginia, in the summer of 1800. Known after its leader as Gabriel's conspiracy, this was a planned attempt to overthrow white hegemony and gain freedom for enslaved blacks. Gabriel Prosser, the leader of the conspiracy, was a young, literate creole slave serving as a blacksmith on Thomas Prosser's plantation in Henrico County, Virginia. Even before the uprising he was respected for his intelligence and courage. He was quite prepared to stand up for his rights as someone with a feisty temperament. In 1799 he spent a month in gaol for biting off part of a white person's left ear after an argument over a stolen hog. To what extent Gabriel was imbued with notions of liberty and freedom propounded by revolutionary white public figures is unknown. But as a literate black he must have been aware of these notions and familiar with the rhetoric of black insurgence that had informed the massive Saint-Domingue slave revolt in the early 1790s. The spread of evangelical preaching in Virginia by Quakers, Baptists and Methodists may also have influenced him; in their prose-lytizing all men, irrespective of race or social status, were viewed as equal by God. It is noteworthy that Gabriel and other black supporters insisted that these religious groups were to be spared any violence during the conspiracy.

The conspiracy was planned in detail – much more, it seems, than had occurred with the Stono Rebellion. It was scheduled to occur in the harvest season so that slaves would not starve and it aimed to recruit thousands of supporters. It had Richmond as its target, not simply because it was a significant urban centre not far from where Gabriel's plantation was situated but because in the vicinity blacks outnumbered whites by about four to one. Elaborate plans were laid to attack Richmond with three columns of black rebels. Advance meetings were held to coordinate strategy. These were not difficult to arrange because at the turn of the nineteenth century most Virginian slave masters exercised a relatively loose hold over their slaves, besides which the common practice of hiring out slaves for work gave them a fair degree of latitude in their everyday movements. Some conspirators were forthright in their intentions. Thus one rebel stated that he had 'nothing more to offer than what General Washington would have had to offer, had he been taken by the British and put to trial. I have adventured my life in endeavouring to obtain the liberty of my countrymen, and am a willing sacrifice in their cause.'[7] After Richmond was taken, Gabriel hoped that the surrounding environs would capitulate to the black insurgents and that he would end up as king of a black-led state.

The actual conspiracy failed to live up to its meticulous organization. Bad luck and lack of unanimity among slaves who knew of the rising in advance contributed to its swift demise. Planned for the night of 30 August 1800, the rising was put off for a day because of severe storms which damaged roads and bridges on the outskirts of Richmond. Gabriel found, as did so many other rebel leaders before and since, that the expected number of followers failed to materialize. He gathered together about 1,000 blacks from six counties to march on Richmond, but this was far less than he had anticipated or needed. Gabriel appears to have had political motives. He marched into Richmond with a banner entitled 'Death or Liberty'. The rising was aborted by the division among the blacks. Some deserted; others informed. The day's delay in putting the arranged plan into action, plus the information relayed from black turncoats to the white militia, enabled Governor James Monroe to call up 600 troops, search out the conspirators, and punish them. Gabriel himself was caught at Norfolk, Virginia, in late September. He was taken back to Richmond, put on trial, and hanged after refusing to name his co-leaders. He was only twenty-four. Another thirty-five rebels were captured and executed. The black informers testified against their fellow slaves at the trials and received no punishment for their actions. Once again a black uprising had failed in North America. But the dominant white class remained uneasy in the Old Dominion. What worried whites in the aftermath of Gabriel's conspiracy was the potential for further slave revolt by acculturated slaves.

Runaways

If rebellions represented the ultimate act of collective resistance by bonded labourers, other types of resistance were more prevalent, none more so than attempts to escape bondage through stealing away from masters. Runaway slaves, servants and convicts were a common feature of North American society in the seventeenth and eighteenth centuries. They usually ran off singly or in pairs; they were often disguised; sometimes they took the tools of their trade to aid their flight. Their aims were diverse. Some wished to escape from North America altogether, usually by jumping aboard ship. Others slipped away for brief periods of time to visit friends or relatives in rural areas. Still others headed for the relative anonymity of large urban centres such as Philadelphia or New York. Permanent runaway communities among slaves were fairly uncommon. Some could be found in the backwoods of the Carolinas or Virginia, where as escapees they would raid plantations for food or forage in wooded areas, but the terrain was not as conducive to such permanent maroon communities as the forests of the interior of Surinam or the mountains of Jamaica. Perhaps the best-known North American maroon hideout was the Great Dismal Swamp, stretching from Norfolk, Virginia, to Edenton in the Albemarle Sound area of North Carolina. A white traveller commented that this area harboured 'prodigious multitudes of every kind of wild beasts peculiar to America, as well as run-away Negroes, who in these horrible swamps are perfectly safe, and with the greatest facility elude the most diligent search of their pursuers'.[8]

American newspapers were full of advertisements for absconders. Rewards were offered for those who collaborated with white masters to find them. Runaways who were caught were subjected to a range of punishments. They could be whipped, placed in iron collars and shackles, or sold. Slaveowners repeatedly complained about the existence of runaways. Some of them, such as George Washington, thought that such fugitives could not be returned successfully to bondage once they had tasted temporary freedom. Masters of convicts and indentured servants were also intensely irritated when their charges fled. The fugitives described in newspapers were just the tip of an iceberg of bonded workers who took flight in an attempt to secure liberty. Other documents referring to runaway bonded labourers indicate that the number was far larger than those advertised. This is unsurprising given that owners would probably only spend money on an advert in cases where a runaway had been absent for a period of at least a month, or where the fugitive was worth recapturing. Most slaves and bonded workers, of course, did not escape from their servitude; but the advertisements for those who did reveal the main characteristics and motives of runaways.

Indentured servant runaways have not been studied intensively, but the work of Sharon Salinger has identified some of their chief characteristics for Pennsylvania.[9] About 6 per cent of Philadelphia's servants ran away in the late colonial period. Some fled to rural areas, or to New York, or jumped aboard ship; others enlisted in the British military forces in wartime. The latter were attracted by the lure of plunder and money but also by the fact that their indentures became void if they remained with the British army. Servant runaways from rural parts of Pennsylvania were more common than fugitives from Philadelphia. Thus two-thirds of the Pennsylvania servants absconding between 1735 and 1744 lived in rural counties; the equivalent proportion for the period 1767–9 was three-quarters. The reasons for the higher incidence of rural runaways is not easy to pin down, but it may be connected to the isolation of these servants and their lack of a support network. Among the urban servant fugitives it was more often the case that an individual would run away with another servant or slave, though as with all bonded escapees, most people stole away by themselves. The penalties for those caught after escape were tough, usually amounting to an extra five days in Pennsylvania for each day of work lost to a master. It seems that the main reason for absconding lay in disputes with masters. Such escapees from the mid-Atlantic colonies declined during the American Revolution. Fewer servants were under indenture by 1777 and those who intended to abscond generally did so in 1775 and 1776, when opportunities were at their best for joining the British forces.

The newspaper press in the eighteenth-century Chesapeake colonies was chockfull of advertisements for runaway convicts. My study of adverts for 816 runaway felons in Maryland in the thirty-year period from 1745 to 1775 indicates their motives and methods in taking flight, and their tenacity in seeking freedom.[10] Convicts deserted from all counties on both shores of Maryland, but 38 per cent of the felons whose residence is given were living in Anne Arundel County and a further 28 per cent in Baltimore County. The chief impulse lying behind convicts fleeing from their owners was to escape their position near the bottom of the social pile, with all the stigmata of being exiled malefactors, thieves, and ne'er-do-wells that were attached to it. William Eddis considered that convicts were 'strained to the utmost to perform their allotted labour'.[11] Apart from general dissatisfaction with their lot, convicts were sometimes also fleeing from brutal treatment by their owners. William Springate had 'the Marks of a Severe Whipping given him lately for breaking into a house' when he absconded from near Baltimore in 1761. Henry Kirk, who vanished from the Baltimore ironworks in 1746, had 'lately been whipt for his Roguery, and the Stripes remain fresh on his back'.[12] Advertisers hinted that another motive of convict runaways was to see people they knew or to hide in places familiar from past experience. Where destinations were stated, they were usually either the large port city of Philadelphia, where fugitives could presumably mingle anonymously with the labouring population, or backcountry areas in Virginia or Maryland, where low population density promised to place runaways beyond the pale of detection.

Running away occurred on horseback, on foot, or by water. The many creeks and rivers of the Chesapeake Bay were used to speed up flight. Felons disguised themselves in different clothes, sometimes wearing wigs; they travelled with the tools of their trade; and they were often armed with pistols, powder, and shot. Of 812 convicts in Maryland c.1745–75 where information is given, 400 (49 per cent) departed by themselves, 236 (29 per cent) left in pairs, 122 (14 per cent) slipped away in groups of three, four and five, but only 54 (7 per cent) left in tandem with indentured servants or slaves. The majority of felons ran away alone or in pairs because this was the most opportune and safest form of escape: self-reliance meant not worrying about accommodating the plans of a fellow deserter with different ideas about remaining at large. Since convicts often had the marks of smallpox or scars and bruises left from iron collars and shackles, and had to carry passes to avoid being detected, vanishing alone was the best way to evade capture. (The Maryland Assembly had passed laws in 1676 and 1715 requiring all servants, including convicts, to carry a pass from their former owner when travelling more than ten miles from home.) Mobility was the defining feature of convict runaways, as it was for slave and servant runaways; and in most parts of British North America the dispersion of most of the population and the fragmentation of the productive system encouraged mobility. But runaways suffered if their attempts at freedom were aborted. William Green, who served a seven-year transportation term in Maryland from 1762 until 1769, wrote that 'if we run away and are taken again, for every hour's absence we must serve twenty-four, for a day, a week, for a week, a month, for a month, a year; and if we steal or commit murder, death is the immediate reward of such actions'.[13]

A notice from the *North Carolina Gazette*, dated 27 April 1775, illustrates some of the main details found in runaway slave advertisements: 'Eloped from the Subscribers on Wednesday the 26th Inst. Two newly imported Men Slaves, named KAUCHEE and BOOHUM, about 6 feet high, and, perhaps, 30 Years of Age. They absconded in Company with three other Slaves about two Months ago, and were taken up at Bread-Creek, about 10 Miles off, and brought back by

William Gailling of that Place, who has since purchased a Wench who was imported with them; from which it is supposed they are lurking about that Neighbourhood. Whoever takes them up and brings them home, shall have Forty Shillings reward from Edward Batchelor & Co.' This is typical in giving the name, height, approximate age, date of flight, suspected destination and level of reward mentioned in such advertisements, and also in containing wording based on hearsay, inference and suspicion. It is just one of thousands of such notices that comprise the main source for analyzing the motives and characteristics of black escapees as seen through the eyes of white masters.

Slaves ran away from their owners for innumerable reasons. Social ties with other blacks were one of the prime motives for absconding. Some African-Americans had experienced separation from family and friends and wished to rejoin them. In Pennsylvania in 1766, for example, a fourteen-year-old slave called Hagar with 'a Scar under one of her Breasts, supposed to be got by Whipping and an iron collar about her Neck' was 'supposed to be harboured in some Negroe Quarter, as her Father and Mother encourage her in these elopments, under a pretence that she is ill used at home'.[14] Male runaways frequently sought out wives, children and parents. A much higher proportion of slaves absconded for these reasons in the Chesapeake than in the Mid-Atlantic region because family ties among the black community were stronger on Virginia and Maryland plantations – a result of the healthy reproductive rate among creole slaves – than in Pennsylvania, New Jersey and Delaware, where slaves were generally held in twos or threes in dispersed rural settlements.

Other reasons why slaves fled included unease about being apprehended after stealing an owner's goods; the desire to escape from cruel masters; the influence of outside agitators; disappointment at not being freed by their owners; and opportunities arising from British military recruitment during the revolutionary war. One such black fugitive was Cuff Dix, who escaped south from Pennsylvania to Virginia only a fortnight after American independence was declared. 'Negroes in general think that Lord Dunmore is contending for their liberty,' his master declared in an advertisement, and 'it is not improbable that said Negroe is on his march to join his Lordship's own black regiment, but it is hoped he will be prevented by some honest Whig from effecting it.'[15] In fact, as Chapter 6 will show, Lord Dunmore's proclamation to free slaves who were willing to flee and join the British army was based as much on the desire to disrupt the slave system and destabilize American society, in the furtherance of military objectives, as on any anti-slavery motive.

Most slave runaways were male. Females usually comprised between one-tenth and one-fifth of absconders in all locales. This ratio can be explained by the greater sense of familial ties found among slave women, notably their reluctance to leave their children. In addition, because more male than female slaves worked as boatmen, ferrymen and labourers on roads and more were hired out, men had greater knowledge of the terrain and more opportunities to escape. The majority of runaways were in their twenties. They were better able to cope with the difficulties of life on the run than older slaves; moreover, middle-aged slaves were more likely to have forged relationships, which might have made them reluctant to move in some cases. In most instances taking flight appears to have been a premeditated act rather a last-minute gamble. A marked seasonal distribution of slave runaways supports this supposition. In North Carolina, for example, the most popular time for African Americans to quit their masters was either during the harvest season from September to November or between February and April, when the slack season ended and spring planting began. In Virginia more slaves ran off in April, when the seasonal pace of tobacco planting increased, than in any other month. In South Carolina the highest incidence of slave absconding occurred in the summer months from May to August, when rice cultivation was particularly rigorous. Innumerable references in runaway advertisements to slaves fleeing with clothes, guns, the tools of their trade, forged passes, and canoes or horses also suggest that plans for freedom were laid before the moment of flight occurred.

In a pioneering study of slave fugitives in Virginia, Gerald W. Mullin argued that acculturated slaves – those with skills – fled in disproportionately large numbers and stood a better chance of remaining at large. His statistics show that between 1736 and 1801 22 per cent of the fugitive slaves in the Old Dominion were either artisans or domestics.[16] But this argument is not persuasive because he does not provide estimates of the proportion of skilled slaves in Virginia's black population as a whole. Contrary to Mullin's view, it may be that the percentage of skilled runaways matched their proportion in the overall slave population, thus reducing the emphasis on acculturated slaves as more likely fugitives. A more salient feature of slave runaways in the plantation southern colonies and states was the differences among African and creole patterns of flight. Philip D. Morgan has shown that the typical African-born slave runaway in Virginia left with one other African whereas in South Carolina half of the Africans who quit plantations left in groups of three or four. This probably reflected the greater preponderance of Africans in the eighteenth-century population of the Lowcountry than in the Chesapeake. Creoles throughout the southern colonies and states generally ran away singly. In the Chesapeake three-quarters of the advertised creole slave runaways left alone; in the Lowcountry the proportion was a half. The main reason for the difference seems to lie in the fact that the South Carolina creoles were less acculturated and therefore less able to cope by themselves.[17]

Notes

1. Quoted in John Berry and Francis Maryson, 'A True Narrative of the Rise, Progresse, and Cessation of the Late Rebellion in Virginia . . .', *Virginia Magazine of History and Biography*, 4 (1897), p. 127.

2. T. H. Breen, 'A Changing Labor Force and Race Relations in Virginia, 1660–1710', *Journal of Social History*, 7 (1973), pp. 3–25, reprinted in his *Puritans and Adventurers: Change and Persistence in Early America* (New York: Oxford University Press, 1980), ch. 7; Edmund S. Morgan, *American Slavery, American Freedom: The Ordeal of Colonial Virginia* (New York: W. W. Norton and Company, 1975), ch. 13.

3. J. H. Easterby (ed.), *The Journal of the Commons House of Assembly, 1741–1742* (Columbia, SC: University of South Carolina Press, 1953), p. 83.

4. *Boston Weekly Newsletter*, 30 Nov. 1739.

5. John K. Thornton, 'African Dimensions of the Stono Rebellion', *American Historical Review*, 96 (1991), pp. 1101–13; Edward A. Pearson, '"A Countryside Full of Flames": A Reconsideration of the Stono Rebellion and Slave Rebelliousness in the Early Eighteenth-Century South Carolina Lowcountry', *Slavery and Abolition*, 17 (1996), pp. 22–50.

6. 'The Journal of William Stephens' in Allen D. Candler and Lucien L. Knight (eds), *The Colonial Records of the State of Georgia*, 26 vols (Atlanta, 1904–16; New York: repr. AMS Press, 1970), iv, p. 592.

7. Robert Sutcliff, *Travels in some Parts of North America, in the Years 1804, 1805, & 1806* (Philadelphia, 1812), p. 50.

8. John Ferdinand Dalziel Smyth, *A Tour of the United States of America*, 2 vols (Dublin: G. Perrin, 1784), ii, p. 102.

9. Sharon V. Salinger, *'To Serve Well and Faithfully': Labor and Indentured Servants in Pennsylvania, 1682–1800* (Cambridge: Cambridge University Press, 1987), pp. 103–7.

10. Kenneth Morgan, 'Convict Runaways in Maryland, 1745–1775', *Journal of American Studies*, 23 (1989), pp. 253–68.

11. Aubrey C. Land (ed.), William Eddis, *Letters from America* (Cambridge, MA: Harvard University Press, 1969), p. 38.

12. *Maryland Gazette*, 4 July 1761, 27 May 1746.
13. William Green, *The Sufferings of William Green* (London, 1774), p. 7.
14. *Pennsylvania Gazette*, 6 Nov. 1766.
15. Ibid., 17 July 1776.
16. Gerald W. Mullin, *Flight and Rebellion: Slave Resistance in Eighteenth-Century Virginia* (New York: Oxford University Press, 1972), pp. 94–6.
17. Philip D. Morgan, *Slave Counterpoint: Black Culture in the Eighteenth-Century Chesapeake and Lowcountry* (Chapel Hill: University of North Carolina Press, 1998), pp. 446–7, 466–7.

CHAPTER 6

Slavery and Freedom in the Revolutionary Era

Dr Samuel Johnson, English Tory and man of letters, put it rhetorically and directly: 'How is it that we hear the loudest *yelps* for liberty among the drivers of negroes?'[1] What he was referring to, of course, was the apparent contradiction between North America's firm commitment to slavery in the revolutionary era and patriots' espousal of liberty, equality and natural rights. This was a dilemma that Americans themselves realized. In 1776 the exiled Thomas Hutchinson, last governor of colonial Massachusetts, challenged the Declaration of Independence, asking how could the delegates from the South 'justify the depriving more than a hundred thousand Africans of their rights to liberty, and the *pursuit of happiness*, and in some degree to their lives, if these rights are so absolutely unalienable'.[2] In 1783 the Quaker David Cooper similarly questioned the libertarian sentiments expressed in the *Declaration*. 'If these solemn *truths*, uttered at such an awful crisis, are *self-evident*: unless we can shew that the African race are not *men*,' he wrote, 'words can hardly express the amazement which naturally arises on reflecting, that the very people who make these pompous declarations are slaveholders, and, by their legislative conduct, tell us, that these blessings were only meant to be the *rights* of *white-men* not of all *men*.'[3]

These quotations are merely the tip of an iceberg of commentary on the interplay between slavery and freedom in the American revolutionary era. Just at the time when Enlightenment emphasis on rational solutions to human difficulties and on progress in human affairs was combined with the natural-rights theory advocated by John Locke – the right of a people to claim their liberty and oppose tyranny – slavery itself was deeply entrenched, especially in the southern states. The institution was so bound up with the economic livelihood of the South that it appeared impregnable. Moreover, the Founding Fathers of the American nation included several prominent Virginians, notably George Washington, Thomas Jefferson and James Madison, who were all slaveholders from a state that included 40 per cent of the entire slaves in the United States at the time of the first Federal Census in 1790. They all argued for liberty for whites but avoided applying the same principle to blacks. Edmund S. Morgan has referred to the contradiction between slavery and freedom in the revolutionary period as the central paradox – and, by implication, the central tragedy – of American History.[4] This chapter explores the complexity of that paradox and assesses how far moves towards black freedom had gone by about 1800.

The Impact of Anti-slavery Ideas

Anti-slavery ideas had begun to make some headway in North America by 1776 and their impact escalated in the following quarter century. Whereas before the mid-eighteenth century scarcely an educated voice raised doubts about the morality of enslaving black people, the situation changed markedly thereafter. Before the 1750s most theologians, lawyers and philosophers condoned slavery uncritically. Increasingly, however, a corpus of anti-slavery ideas gained currency and had to be addressed by statesmen and the educated public. The first major landmark in the growth of these ideas was not a British or an American source but the work of a French *philosophe*. Montesquieu, in his *L'Esprit des Lois* (1748), included an oblique attack on slavery and the slave trade that proved highly influential in changing other intellectuals' views. Neither slaveholders nor slaves could, in Montesquieu's view, act in a morally virtuous way, the former because they exercised unlimited authority, the latter because their actions lacked fully independent choice. Montesquieu argued that where slavery existed, laws must be introduced to guard against its nature. Scottish Enlightenment philosophers, including Adam Smith, took up the anti-slavery mantle in the 1750s and 1760s by arguing that slavery was an unsatisfactory condition that denied a certain category of people the right to political and civil happiness. The conservative English jurist William Blackstone similarly attacked slavery. He argued against the hereditary arguments for possessing slaves, contesting the view that they were property that could be willed from one generation to the next. He also denied the legality of the captivity or sale of slaves. Among religious groups, condemnation of slaveholding increased. Methodists such as John Wesley and Francis Asbury exhorted against the immorality of slaveholding. Quakers denounced slavery and the slave trade as wicked. The evangelical wing of the Church of England opposed black bondage by emphasizing the

Christian duty to behave benevolently, to accept the bounty of God's providence, and to fulfil the goal of progressive revelation. This entailed bringing peace and plenty to nations where moral worth had been demonstrated and destruction and war to those acting in an immoral way.

Many of these ideas, as suggested, emanated in the first place from Europe rather than America, but they were widely discussed and circulated throughout the transatlantic world via correspondence, the spread of printed literature, visits to North America, speeches, sermons and lectures. The Quakers, in particular, played a crucial role in spreading the anti-slavery message because of their well-developed transatlantic links. Prominent American Friends such as Anthony Benezet and John Woolman publicized the cause both at home and on visits to Britain. The Religious Society of Friends believed in pacifism and condemned warfare; they were therefore opposed to the capture of slaves in tribal conflicts in west Africa. They believed that all people were equal in the eyes of God, whatever their skin colour and worldly status. Quakers banned their members from engaging in the slave trade; they also disapproved of Friends owning slaves. Yet even for the Quakers the crusade against slaveholding did not come easily. In the American heartland of eighteenth-century Quakerism – Pennsylvania and New Jersey – Friends strived for generations until about 1770 before it was accepted that slaveholding among their members should be banned. The radical wing of Quakers in the Delaware Valley found it difficult to persuade their moderate colleagues to go further than expelling slaveowners from the Society of Friends and to work together to end oppression for American blacks. By the time of the American Revolution, Quaker philanthropy towards free blacks was limited, being based on gradualist, paternalist and segregationist policies.

The sea change in approaches to slavery that gathered apace in the quarter century after 1750 – exemplified by many more individuals and groups than can be mentioned here – stood to make some impact on the Declaration of Independence. But the relationship of slavery to that founding script of American nationhood reveals the ambiguities of tackling the 'peculiar institution' publicly in the new United States of America. 'We hold these Truths to be self-evident,' the document stated, 'that all Men are created equal, that they are endowed by their Creator with certain unalienable Rights, that among these are Life, Liberty, and the Pursuit of Happiness.' Behind the seemingly progressive language, however, the broad concepts espoused had a more limited meaning for contemporaries. 'Men', in the political discourse of the time, referred to adult white males. 'Unalienable Rights' meant natural rights for white men. 'Liberty' was to be reserved to those enjoying 'the Pursuit of Happiness': white, propertied males. Blacks had an inferior position in the pyramid of human societies; they were consequently disqualified from membership in the political world. Jefferson, who penned the document, had included clauses on slavery in the original draft of the Declaration. He had blamed King George III himself for waging 'a cruel war against human nature itself, violating its most sacred rights of life and liberty in the persons of a distant people who never offended him & carrying them into slavery in another hemisphere'. But this statement ignored the ready importation of black slaves from Africa by those in the North American colonies since the seventeenth century. It was omitted from the published version of the Declaration because it would have created problems with the southern states at a time when the new republic needed a unified beginning. At meetings of the Continental Congress, a conclave that represented all thirteen colonies except Georgia, it proved a highly contentious issue. The result was that Jefferson dropped all references to slavery in the final version of the document, thereby postponing reference to it in public statements of political principles for more than a decade.

Slavery and the War of Independence

Slavery was already a contentious issue among antislavery supporters and American public figures when independence was declared on 4 July 1776. One might expect therefore that the revolutionary war, and the position of blacks during the conflict, would trigger changes in the treatment of slaves in North America. And so it proved. But attitudes towards blacks in the War of Independence and the actions of slaves during the conflict reveal the complexity of the issues at stake. Both the British and American forces grappled with the question of whether to recruit black troops. They were well aware of how such enlistment would affect the plantation system, the pattern of racial discrimination and the desires of enslaved blacks for freedom. In November 1775 the British took the initiative in recruiting blacks when the governor of Virginia, Lord Dunmore, issued a proclamation offering freedom to American slaves who would flee from captivity to aid the British army. Dunmore's proclamation was preceded by several blacks approaching him a few months beforehand and offering to join the British forces and take up arms. It was an attempt by the British to manipulate the military situation; they had no real intention of granting freedom to slaves. Rather, the proclamation aimed to upset the stability of the American slave system and make the planters worry about their security. Later in the war, another British initiative raised black hopes of emancipation. In June 1779 General Henry Clinton proclaimed from his headquarters at Philipsburg, New York, that blacks aiding the Continental army would be sold for the benefit of their captors while those who deserted and aided the British military would be granted full security to follow occupations of their choice. Once again, however, this was not a humane offer of freedom for slaves but an attempt to disrupt American patriots psychologically and in terms of manpower.

The American forces were opposed initially to arming slaves for the revolutionary war, though some blacks had served in militia units (mainly in the northern states) at the outset of the conflict. A few days after being appointed commander-in-chief of the Continental army, George Washington issued orders against enlisting blacks. In November 1775, the Continental Congress formally declared all blacks ineligible for military service. But the situation soon changed. American military commanders and politicians saw Dunmore's initiative drawing blacks into British ranks, while Washington came around to the view that the outcome of the war depended 'on which side can arm the Negroes the faster'.[5] By the end of December 1775, Washington was willing to support the enlistment of free blacks. He recommended this action to Congress. In January 1776 Congress resolved that free blacks who had served faithfully in the army at Cambridge, Massachusetts – where the Council of War was then based – could enlist but no others: slaves were excluded from American armies. Yet a subsequent manpower shortage among the American forces led by 1777 to free blacks and slaves joining a number of mixed regiments, mainly in the northern states.

The impact of the revolutionary war on American blacks was not confined to how they were deployed or put aside for military service. The length of the conflict (seven years) and the internal discord that beset the southern states (especially after 1778) meant that various options were open to blacks: they could flee from their masters, resist the plantation system, challenge their chattel condition, engage in conspiracies, join the British forces, or remain neutral. In fact, each of these courses was taken. Already by the summer of 1775 a slave insurrection scare occurred in the Cape Fear area of North Carolina. A threatened black insurrection in St Bartholomew parish, South Carolina, followed in the spring of 1776. Throughout the war other attempts at revolt were encouraged by expectations of freedom, for slaves, though largely illiterate, became familiar with revolutionary notions of freedom and equality through eavesdropping, table talk and the spread of news orally. Some slaves participated in acts of violence against people and property; some fled plantations for the greater anonymity of towns and ports; some aided the armed forces of both belligerents as plunderers and capturers of deserters; some remained neutral on plantations, waiting to see which side would gain the military advantage. There was no set pattern to slave behaviour, but the War of Independence opened up the range of active choices enslaved blacks could take in search of liberty.

Perhaps the most telling aspect of slave behaviour during the war was the sheer numbers who used opportunities to quit slavery. Though the evidence is incomplete and subject to a degree of error, something like 10,000 slaves from Georgia (two-thirds of its pre-war slave population) and 20,000 slaves from South Carolina were lost during the war. The biggest exodus was reserved for 1782 when white loyalists and the British army quitting Savannah, Charleston and St Augustine took about 20,000 slaves with them. Some estimates reckon that the total scale of the flight of blacks from the United States during the war was 80,000 people. Washington regarded this exodus as a violation of the preliminary articles of peace signed at Paris on 30 November 1782. He hoped for the recovery of American blacks who had escaped with the British. But in meeting Sir Guy Carleton, the British commander-in-chief, at Orangetown, New York, on 6 May 1783, Washington accepted the loss of slaves manumitted by the British forces before the provisional peace treaty was signed to prevent the resumption of war. The blacks who fled the United States of America found new homes in Britain, Africa and parts of the British Empire (with Nova Scotia and some of the Caribbean islands being favoured destinations).

If the revolutionary war had actually achieved little in improving the situation of those who remained slaves in the United States, the ferment of libertarian ideas and the prolonged military conflict had emphasized that expectations were high among blacks and anti-slavery supporters for moves towards black freedom. To achieve this goal it would be necessary for change to occur at the legislative level in the individual states or through policies agreed by the Continental Congress. It would also be vital for prominent military leaders and statesmen to realize the anomaly of the continued existence of slavery in a free republic and to articulate their views in public. At the legislative level, little happened. True, in 1778 the Virginia House of Delegates banned the further importation of African slaves. But this, far from being a humanitarian gesture, was designed to protect Virginia from an oversupply of new slaves in a context where demographic growth among creole slaves in Virginia was flourishing. Virginia, in fact, had imported very few new slaves from 1770 onwards. The major opportunity that the Continental Congress had to issue public statements about slavery occurred with the drafting of the Articles of Confederation in 1781. Yet this document, a set of guidelines for the loose cooperation of states, ignored slavery. The Continental Congress did not have the constitutional power to ensure provisions would be carried out by individual states. The immediate need was for firmer arrangements dealing with military, governmental and financial affairs, all covered in the Articles and more pressing concerns to statesmen than opening up the hornet's nest of what to do about slavery and the slave trade.

The Founding Fathers and Slavery

The individuals who could have made a difference to public perceptions of slavery in the revolutionary era were the Founding Fathers of the nation. An understanding of their limited willingness to move towards an anti-slavery position can be gained from consideration of slaveholders who were either leading military and political figures in the revolutionary period or philosopher-statesmen of the constitutional foundations of American liberty. In other words, a discussion of the Virginia triumvirate Washington, Madison and Jefferson can illuminate the complexity of the issues surrounding slavery and abolitionism in the last quarter of the eighteenth century. Washington's leadership as commander-in-chief of the Continental army in the revolutionary war and first president of the USA gave him the most elevated military and political positions in the young American republic and vantage points of great influence where the problem of slavery had to be addressed. Madison, as co-author of the *Federalist* papers, drafter of the Bill of Rights, and later fourth president, had the public position and intellectual capacity to offer a solution to the Pandora's box of slavery. And

Jefferson, as author of the Declaration of Independence, governor of Virginia and third president, also had the platform, in public life and through his writings, to offer a lead to the nation on slavery. All of them, as we shall see, left decisive action on racial issues to later generations. Disentangling their varied views on slavery illuminates why the continued existence of black bondage was such an intractable problem in the United States.

Washington, Madison and Jefferson had various things in common with regard to slavery besides their birth in the Old Dominion. They all inherited slaves from their parents or other close kin. They all became substantial slaveholders: Washington at Mount Vernon, adjacent to the Potomac River; Madison at Montpelier plantation in Orange County; Jefferson at Monticello, the home he built near Charlottesville. They were all interested in deploying slave labour efficiently during a period when the Chesapeake economy needed less slave labour on tobacco plantations because of diversification into grain production. They appear to have treated their slaves benevolently on the whole, respecting personal relationships forged among the blacks under their control. Yet they were all prepared to punish recalcitrant slaves, condemn runaways, and insist on hard work and close supervision of their labour force. Moreover, they made their home in a state where social prestige depended on acting as patriarchs in their own households and thriving as successful landholders. Even so, they reacted to the problems of slavery in distinctive ways.

Washington expressed a fair amount of dissatisfaction with the slave system. Before the War of Independence, he purchased slaves at Mount Vernon to support his family expenses but in 1778 he noted that he had surplus slaves on his farms and longed to get rid of them. He also expressed great irritation at slaves who quit Mount Vernon, considering that those who ran away could not be returned to useful, obedient work. He seems to have profited little, if at all, from keeping slaves, and Mount Vernon was in considerable debt towards the end of his life. By 1786, in a phrase that he repeated, he referred to slaves as 'that species of property which I have no inclination to possess'.[6] The problem of whether to arm blacks during the revolutionary war was, as explained above, something that forced Washington to articulate his views on slavery. Moreover, his public positions, military service and extensive travel gave him a broad view of the role of blacks, both free and enslaved, in the new nation. In the light of his dissatisfaction with slave labour at Mount Vernon and this broader awareness of the implications of continued slaveholding in the United States, it is legitimate to ask why he did not free his own slaves in his lifetime or advocate anti-slavery openly.

Washington's public cautiousness on the question of slavery stemmed not merely from temperamental reserve but from his sense of the divisive nature of slavery in the young republic. On several public occasions where he could have spoken out against slavery he chose not to do so: this is true of his presence at the Constitutional Convention in 1787 and it remained the case during his presidency. At Philadelphia in the summer of 1787 he acted as chairman of the convention, in which capacity he could enter discussions, but there were occasions when he joined fellow delegates on the floor and, in theory, could have debated slavery and other issues. During his presidency, he hardly commented on the fears raised in 1791 by the massive slave rebellion in Saint-Domingue, and he signed the fugitive slave law of 1793 that enabled slaveholders to cross state lines to recapture runaways. When Washington gave his farewell address in 1796, he remained silent on slavery. No doubt he wanted to give priority to presenting a harmonious message in handing on his executive position, and was aware that his position as first president of the United States would earmark his words for posterity.

In private meetings and in his correspondence, however, Washington expressed increasing, if cautious, sympathy for abolitionism from the end of the revolutionary war onwards. He privately agreed with the abolitionist sentiments expressed by two prominent Methodist visitors to Mount Vernon, Thomas Coke and Francis Asbury. He confessed in a letter to superintendent of finance Robert Morris that he wanted to see a plan adopted for the abolition of slavery in the United States, but that legislative authority was needed to do so. He hoped that the Virginia legislature would abolish slavery 'by slow, sure, & imperceptable degrees'.[7] If slavery continued to divide America, Washington wrote to his Attorney General Edmund Randolph that 'he had made up his mind to move and be of the northern'.[8] This comment reveals his sensitivity over slavery. In an undated memorandum he noted that 'to lay a foundation to prepare the rising generation for a destiny different from that in which they [the slaves] were born afforded some satisfaction to my mind'.[9] In old age Washington thought carefully about what to with his slaves. He dealt with their plight, and implicitly signalled his intentions for the American republic, in his last will and testament by decreeing that his slaves should be freed but only after his wife's death. At the end of his life Washington owned 124 slaves plus 153 dower slaves that he had no legal right to free; and he did not want to break up long-standing personal relationships between enslaved blacks from both groups. Washington was the only Founding Father to free a significant number of his slaves.

James Madison appears to have been uncomfortable with slavery from his young manhood, for he contemplated acquiring new land outside Virginia that would enable him to avoid using slaves. But this plan never came to fruition: it was probably unrealistic to cast off the property, land and labour he had inherited in Virginia. Madison consistently felt a repugnance for the continuation of slavery in a young republic founded on principles of natural rights. There is no doubt that this troubled his conscience. Throughout his public career he struggled to accept the continued existence of slavery in the United States and pursued schemes that he thought would eradicate it, but these all led to nothing. In 1780, while serving in the Continental Congress, he responded to a Virginia bill offering slaves as a recruiting bounty by advocating the liberation of blacks and their enlistment in the Continental army. This 'would certainly be more consonant to the principles of liberty', he noted, 'which ought never to be lost sight of in a contest for liberty'.[10] His suggestion fell on deaf ears.

In 1785 Madison spoke in the Virginia Assembly in support of Jefferson's bill for the gradual abolition of slavery, but the measure was rejected. At the Constitutional Convention in 1787, Madison hoped to see the foreign slave trade banned but he had to accept the compromise position that the traffic would not be outlawed constitutionally for twenty years. While serving in the first Congress, Madison reflected on a colonizing plan, written by a Virginian, to settle blacks on the coast of Africa. He saw merit in this proposal, thinking that it 'might afford the best hope yet presented of putting an end to the slavery in which not less than 600,000 unhappy negroes are now involved'. Such a plan to establish a haven for former slaves in Africa 'might induce the humanity of Masters, and by degrees both the humanity & policy of the Governments, to forward the abolition of Slavery in America'.[11] In later years he again advocated schemes for the removal of slaves to Africa, something that also appealed to Jefferson. The thinking behind these proposals was that white Americans were not yet ready for the racial adjustment necessary to accept free blacks on an equal footing within the United States; therefore colonization for the blacks overseas seemed the solution. Yet schemes put forward in the early nineteenth century to promote black resettlement in Liberia, a new colony on the west coast of Africa, never stood a realistic chance of relocating significant numbers of slaves.

Madison therefore hoped for slave emancipation but could not envisage how this would arise given the racial superiority his fellow white Americans felt towards slaves and free blacks: adjustment to a racially integrated society seemed to him impossible by the 1820s and 1830s. He himself never made any public – or, as far as we know, private – statements about the inferiority of black people and yet, despite his eminence in American public life, he never proposed a solution to slavery in the United States. He believed in gradual slave emancipation, but with no time-scale specified, and considered that masters would have to be compensated for the loss of slave labour because the Constitution confirmed that slaves were property. Madison, like Jefferson, lived for more than two decades after Washington's death but neither came round to freeing significant numbers of slaves in their wills. In Madison's case, practical considerations concerning his younger spouse made him shy away from granting freedom to his slave charges: maintaining slaves would help her financially after his death. But Madison also recognized the limited acceptance of even free blacks in Virginia by the 1830s. This also influenced his decision to preserve the enslaved status of his own black workers for his beneficiaries. Though this conceivably helped those slaves to gain decent treatment, it did nothing to resolve their continued immiseration in bondage.

Of the three Virginian Founding Fathers discussed here, Thomas Jefferson was the one who displayed the most complex reactions to slavery and the one whose relationship to slavery has proved most controversial among historians. Persons no less prominent than Abraham Lincoln and Martin Luther King have drawn inspiration from Jefferson's supposed anti-slavery creed. Among historians, some applaud Jefferson's statements on slavery as helping to put the institution of slavery on the defensive. Recognizing the bravery of speaking publicly about slavery when it was a highly divisive issue in the early republic, such commentators regard Jefferson's stance on slavery as a genuine, if pained, acknowledgement of the limits to freedom in the new nation. Others take a more critical position. For instance, William W. Freehling has referred to Jefferson's conditional anti-slavery mentality as characteristic of someone who could never argue for ending slavery without imposing terms that could not be met.[12] Others have laid bare Jefferson's negrophobia and have argued that Jefferson was the one Founding Father who had repeated opportunities to influence public opinion against slavery but who continually hedged his bets; in other words, he was not genuinely an advocate of anti-slavery at all.

In Jefferson's writings, there are undoubted expressions of negrophobia: something, as mentioned above, that is not found in any statements by Washington or Madison. In his *Notes on the State of Virginia* (1784), Jefferson wrote about the intellectual inferiority of Negroes; he also expressed his fears about miscegenation and the potential for violence by blacks against whites. Blacks should not be incorporated into the state because white prejudices and slave resentment 'will probably never end but in the extermination of the one or the other race'. He thought that some form of colonization would place the slave 'beyond the reach of mixture' so that he would not stain 'the blood of his master'.[13] Such racism was and is deplorable, and it is unsurprising that Jefferson did not want his *Notes* circulated publicly. When the great Saint-Domingue slave rebellion erupted in the heady days of French revolutionary fervour, Jefferson wrote of his fears that the spirit of revolt, and bloody consequences, would spread to the United States; and in his statements on the revolt there is again an unequivocal sense of negrophobia. Jefferson believed that free blacks and whites could not coexist peacefully in the early republic partly for racial reasons but also because he believed in an agrarian ideal of a republic of yeomen farmers. In such a social and political system, farmers would be independent and free of debt; only then could they act virtuously as citizens. Unfortunately, this view of American society had severe implications for Jefferson's own slaves and for slavery as an institution; for while the sage of Monticello remained a debtor he could not free his slaves, unless he wanted to face financial ruin, but equally slaves could not act independently and virtuously because they were white men's chattel property.

It would be wrong to suggest that Jefferson did not speak against slavery or advocate steps for it to be eradicated. Nevertheless he changed his position over time, and made contradictory statements on the problem. Though in his *Notes on the State of Virginia* he cast aspersions on the capacity of black people for learning, he later wrote letters in which he argued that blacks were potentially the equal of whites should their circumstances improve. In 1786 he underscored the miserable condition of slaves but in 1814 stated that American slaves 'are better fed . . . , warmer clothed, and labor less than the journeymen or day-laborers of England'.[14] On several occasions, he broached the notions of gradual emancipation and slave manumission but always withdrew from acting on these views. As early as 1769 he had supported a bill in the Virginia House of Burgesses to allow private manumission of slaves. After this was defeated, Jefferson remained silent on the issue in public for the rest of his life. While governor of Virginia (1776–9), Jefferson proposed legislation for free blacks, white women with mixed race children, and manumitted slaves, but the legislature defeated his proposal. In the spring of 1783, it is true, he privately suggested a gradual emancipation programme for Virginia; but he made no public statement on the issue and left the matter for the Virginia General Assembly to deal with.

Jefferson's solution to the continuation of slavery in the early republic was similar to Madison's: slaves should be freed and sent back to settle in Africa. Jefferson did not envisage a harmonious social setting in the South between whites and freed slaves; he also did not regard free blacks as voters or citizens because he thought they would endanger the republic. Jefferson's famous statement about slavery at the time of the Missouri Compromise (1821) expressed his inability to act to resolve the paradox of slavery and freedom in a land of liberty: 'We have the wolf by the ear, and we can neither hold him, nor safely let him go. Justice is in one scale, and self-preservation in the other.'[15] Jefferson's eloquence is memorable but words are not deeds: one senses that Jefferson would have enjoyed playing the role of Hamlet up to the end of the fourth act of Shakespeare's tragedy but would have made his excuses and left the theatre in the interval before the fifth act began.

Space precludes further discussion of the complexity of Jefferson's attitudes towards race and slavery. But his reputation on these issues has recently been severely compromised by evidence about the nature of his relationship with the mulatto Sally Hemings, the half-sister of his wife Martha. The story that Jefferson fathered slave children by Hemings was first published in the Richmond *Recorder* in 1802. Two centuries of speculation on this issue have followed. Historians who regard Jefferson as troubled over racial issues but sincerely hoping that slavery could be eradicated have discounted the tale; they have added that Jefferson's personal control over his emotions – a common theme in assessments of his character – was such that the relationship with Hemings could not have happened. Critics of Jefferson have, on the contrary, accused him of hiding this relationship from posterity, and have cited circumstantial evidence that makes the liaison at least a strong possibility. The true situation will never be determined. But recent DNA tests have shown that at least one of Hemings's five children born at Monticello was probably Jefferson's son, though clearly the genetic testing cannot rule out the possibility that the son's father was another Jefferson male.[16]

The American Government and Slavery

While the young American republic remained a loose conglomeration of states, little could be decided at national level about the future of slavery and the slave trade. The Articles of Confederation, agreed by the Continental Congress in 1781, included no clauses pertaining to these subjects. Under its provisions, individual states retained their sovereignty. Thus the importation of slaves could continue legally; only individual states had the right to ban the traffic. But Congress can claim one accomplishment relating to slavery and its jurisdiction: namely the Northwest Ordinance of 1787. This law established the Northwest Territory and was mainly concerned with laying down the stages for setting up states in that domain; but it also forbade slavery legal protection inside its boundaries. In so doing, the ordinance had parallels with the British government's attempt to exclude slavery from Georgia in 1735: both were legislative acts confined to particular territories but with no overall challenge to the institution of North American slavery.

Trying to understand the motives behind the passing of the Northwest Ordinance has puzzled historians. Some regard it as the first liberal measure enacted by the American government against slavery at a time when it was difficult to exclude slavery from any North American territory. It ensured that slavery as it spread westwards would not be permitted in the Northwest Territory – the future states of Ohio, Indiana, Illinois, Wisconsin and Michigan – by settlers moving up from trans-Appalachian regions, notably the future states of Kentucky and Tennessee. At the time the Ordinance was passed, of course, no-one could predict precisely the scale or movement of American internal migration to the west. Equally, though, few public figures were in any doubt that there would be a substantial westward 'push'. Given that in the Southwest Ordinance (1784) Jefferson's proposal to prohibit slavery in all western territories after 1800 had failed – but only by one congressional vote – it was an achievement to restrict the future spread of slavery in one part of the Union. And the lack of debate on Article VI of the Northwest Ordinance – the slavery clause – was probably a blessing in disguise: detailed consideration of the status of slaves already living in the Northwest Territory might have sabotaged the law.

Others suggest, on the contrary, that the failure of the Northwest Ordinance to include any enforcement clauses and its stipulation that fugitive slaves 'may be lawfully reclaimed and conveyed to the person claiming' them illustrated the lukewarm commitment to anti-slavery of the committee that passed the measure. This interpretation concludes that the words of Article VI sound idealistic but had little practical effect. Implicit in this view is that full-fledged discussion should have taken place over the status of slaves already living in the Northwest Territory and that legislative enactments and enforcement were necessary to make the slavery clause of the Ordinance meaningful. Two points, however, are worth remembering. First, Article VI was a brief clause inserted literally at the last minute in the drafting of the measure. Second, the Ordinance was approved by Congress in New York on 13 July 1787, a day after the Constitutional Convention in Philadelphia adopted the three-fifths compromise over slavery for taxation and representation purposes (discussed below) that was the crucial turning point in the constitutional debate over slavery. As Staughton Lynd has suggested, there may have been a sectional compromise involving Congress and the Convention: southerners could have supported the Ordinance in return for the agreement that new states from the Northwest would soon be created to maintain southern security in the proposed new House of Representatives.[17] But this intelligent link between the discussions over the Northwest Ordinance and the Constitutional Convention cannot be proven definitively.

Other reasons why southerners supported the Northwest Ordinance are not absolutely clearcut. But it seems that they felt several advantages had been gained as a result of this measure. It appeared to imply that slavery was secure south of the Ohio River. Southern congressmen might not have expected the prohibition to be permanent or effective. It would limit the territory in which slave-grown staples could be cultivated and thereby cut down competition with the existing southern economy. Furthermore, possibly both southern and northern congressmen needed an Ordinance that would be accepted by the Ohio Land Company, scheduled to purchase five million acres of land in the Northwest Territory.

The most significant move by the American government over slavery came, of course, with the debates held during the Constitutional Convention. The future principles of the United States government were the core of the convention's work, as the American republic, weakened in terms of finance and defence by the deficiencies of the Articles of Confederation, settled down to the task of defining American constitutional principles in a written document. There was no national consensus about the need for stronger government and fierce divisions emerged between Federalists and Anti-federalists. When the fifty-five delegates to the Constitutional Convention met on 25 May, slavery did not appear to be high on their agenda. Indeed, during the early proceedings it was a subject that caused little friction whenever it was raised. Over the course of the summer, however, slavery became a central issue of debate over such matters as the form of representation for the new House of Representatives and the structure of the central government. Heated disputes arose, and for a time it seemed that the issue of slavery would lead to the break up of the convention. Political compromises were reached to accommodate the sensitivities of the two southernmost states over slavery, and when the convention adjourned on 17 September 1787 the draft Federal Constitution included explicit sanctions for slavery in at least five articles and indirect protection of slavery in at least ten other clauses.

The two major issues pertaining to slavery and the slave trade at the Constitutional Convention were the question of how to count slaves for purposes of representation and taxation within the federal government and what to do about the future importation of slaves into the Union. Both issues were discussed in detail without the word 'slave' being used in any of the written documentation – a recognition that the word, as one contemporary put it, 'might be odious to the ears of Americans'.[18] The federal ratio – the notion that five slaves should be equivalent to three white people – had first been proposed by the Confederation Congress in 1783 as part of a programme for the national government to raise revenue from the states. It had not then been adopted because it failed to receive the unanimous approval of all the states. It was now hammered out in debate as the way in which southern states could guarantee that their chattel property would be recognized for purposes of national taxation and representation in the House of Representatives, ensuring their political strength in that chamber for the foreseeable future.

After first being raised at the Constitutional Convention on 11 June 1787, the three-fifths clause was regularly debated over the next three months. Delegates from South Carolina and Georgia – where slavery was a central economic institution – were adamant that this clause should be passed or they would not vote in favour of the Constitution. On 11 July the three-fifths clause failed by a vote of four to six. On the following day, when it was tied to taxation for the first time, it passed by a vote of six to two with two states divided. Eventually it was incorporated into Article 1, Section 2 of the Constitution: 'Representatives and direct taxes shall be apportioned among the several States which may be included within this Union, according to their respective Numbers, which shall be determined by adding to the whole Number of free Persons, including those bound to Service for a Term of Years, and excluding Indians not taxed, three-fifths of all other persons.'

The debates over the foreign slave trade mainly occurred during August 1787. There was bitter sectional acrimony over this matter but a compromise was reached whereby the South Carolina delegation supported the commerce in return for New England supporting protection for the slave trade. On 25 August the committee proposed that Congress should have no power to interfere with the slave trade for twenty-one years but taxes could be levied on imported Africans. Maryland, Georgia, South Carolina and the New England states combined to secure this arrangement by a vote of seven to four. The compromise became Article 1, Section 9 of the Constitution: 'The Migration or Importation of such Persons as any of the States now existing shall think proper to admit, shall not be prohibited by the Congress prior to the Year one thousand eight hundred and eight but a Tax or duty may be imposed on such Importation, not exceeding ten dollars for each Person.' After this clause had been agreed in principle, a fugitive slave clause – similar to the one in the Northwest Ordinance – was drafted and included in the final document without, perhaps surprisingly, any debate. This became Article 4, Section 2 of the Constitution: 'No Person held to Service or Labour in one State, under the Laws thereof, escaping into another, shall, in Consequence of any Law or Regulation therein, be discharged from such Service or Labour, but shall be delivered up on Claim of the Party to whom such Service may be due.'

Slavery was a significant component of the debates within the states over the ratification of the Constitution. These mainly took place between late September 1787 and late July 1788, when New York's approval guaranteed that the Constitution had enough national support to be workable. Some interesting patterns emerge from considering how slavery and the slave trade were discussed during the ratification process. On the three-fifths clause, a clear sectional divide between New England and the southern states was evident. New Englanders feared that Article 1, Section 2 would lead to the South being over-represented in Congress. 'Tell me, if you can,' one northern writer asked, 'why a southern *negro*, in his present debased condition, is any more entitled to representation, than a northern *Bullock*? Both are mere pieces of property – and nothing more!'[19] Yet there was unanimity in the South over this clause precisely because of the political advantage it offered in the lower house of Congress. Madison argued in *The Federalist* that slaves were regarded by the framers of the Constitution as both property and persons, and that compromise over representation was justified because slaves were 'debased by servitude below the equal level of free inhabitants which regards the *slave* as divested of two fifths of the *man*'.[20]

No consensus arose among the states with regard to the Constitution's provisions over the foreign slave trade and, as a result, there was extensive and inconclusive debate over that matter. Critics objected to Article 1, Section 9 on moral and Christian grounds and saw it as inconsistent with republican principles and justice. In New England and the Middle States it was feared that Congress's lack of immediate power to deal with the foreign slave trade protected southern states' rights. Positive appraisals suggested that the Constitutional Convention had gone as far as it could on this matter; that South Carolina and Georgia were thus kept within the Union; and that Congress would discourage the slave trade up to 1808. The fugitive slave clause elicited little discussion. All in all, the South did well out of the compromise over slavery and the slave trade in the framing and ratification of the Constitution. But though the Founding Fathers worked assiduously to create a Constitution that would preserve national unity, the ambiguity of the clauses dealing with slavery and the slave trade meant that Americans, though they voted for ratification, had signed up to a document that left many crucial issues associated with slavery unresolved. No wonder that Gouverneur Morris, a Pennsylvania delegate at the Constitutional Convention and an insightful commentator on slavery, referred to domestic slavery as 'the curse of heaven on the States where it prevailed'.[21]

Slavery in American Regions during the Revolutionary Era

If the Founding Fathers' treatment of slavery was ambiguous and, at best, an equivocal commitment to abolitionism, a similarly complex situation characterized the regional development of black life in the revolutionary era. During the American Revolution all northern states, with the exception of New York and New Jersey, took steps to eradicate slavery. Legislative, judicial and constitutional action against slavery occurred in Massachusetts and New Hampshire and gradual abolition laws were passed in Pennsylvania (1780), Rhode Island (1784) and Connecticut (1784). In New York and New Jersey, where opposition to anti-slavery was more virulent, gradual emancipation bills did not pass the state legislatures until 1799 and 1804. Though the essential laws to free blacks were therefore set in train in the northern states in the last quarter of the eighteenth century, these moves towards black freedom were very gradual indeed: many statutes granted freedom only for future-born children of slaves at ages between twenty-one and twenty-eight. This meant that in most northern states freedom for the majority of slaves did not occur until after the turn of the nineteenth century.

In the northern port cities, free black communities were forged between 1770 and 1800 as slavery became more of a southern rather than a national institution. The proportion of free blacks living in both New York City and Philadelphia increased in that period: a result partly of manumissions accorded to blacks already living there and partly of migration of free blacks from the Upper South. Free blacks found work in the maritime industries and as domestic servants. They began to construct their own cohesive communities based around membership of black churches, the creation of black schools and the formation of nuclear families. The black churches established tended to be evangelical in their form of worship; they stemmed from the Free African societies established in the northern port cities in the late 1780s and early 1790s. As a personal riposte to their former slave status, free blacks often changed the names given to them by white masters; they replaced African day names, classical names and place names with English and biblical names for themselves and their children.

These positive developments for blacks were nevertheless the result of struggle. They took years to achieve. By 1811 Philadelphia had nine black schools, New York City only one. By 1813 there were only six black churches in Philadelphia and two in New York City. Achieving a stable, nuclear family life only came slowly in the wake of the revolution. Poverty and dislocation accompanied black migration to the northern port cities and freed blacks remained in their white masters' houses until they had the money to set up home independently. Yet, despite the problems encountered, free blacks in urban settings began to build up a more autonomous, fraternal social sphere for their families than had been the case under slavery. Black preachers, in particular, played an important role in interpreting the stories, symbols and events of the Bible to bolster the daily lives of black folk and provided a means by which blacks – both free and slave – could participate actively in an institution that gave meaning to their lives.

Free blacks were also a part of life in the Chesapeake by the late eighteenth century. One third of the free blacks in the USA lived in that region by 1810. But they only flourished in certain areas, more often in Maryland than in Virginia and, within the Old Dominion, more frequently in the upper reaches of the state, within reach of the Potomac, than in tidewater and Piedmont areas. Thus by 1810 some 20 per cent of Maryland's black population were freedmen but only 7 per cent of Virginia's. From 1782 onwards Virginia had a law whereby masters could free slaves individually or in groups, whereas previously, dating back to 1723, only the governor and council could free a slave in the colony. In the 1790s hundreds of Virginia masters began to free their slaves, but they usually only manumitted small numbers. Even exceptions to this rule, such as Robert Carter of Nomini Hall, arranged to manumit slaves over a long time span (in Carter's case some 509 slaves over twenty-two years, not all of whom were in fact eventually freed).

Thus the growth of a free black population in parts of the Chesapeake in the period 1770–1800 was accompanied by an expansion of slavery in other parts of the region as the peculiar institution became an ever more deeply entrenched southern hallmark. In 1785 a proposal to abolish slavery within Virginia was defeated in the House of Delegates. Extensive pro-slavery petitions were drawn up in several Virginia counties in the same year. In 1793 Virginia prohibited the immigration of free blacks into the state, and opponents of manumission in the state were vociferous. At the time all but one of the legislators in the House of Delegates were slaveholders. In 1806 the Assembly, worried by the impact of Gabriel's slave conspiracy in 1800, restricted manumission. Increasing numbers of whites became slaveholders in western Virginia in the late eighteenth century as slavery expanded into land that had previously been unsettled. As Richard S. Dunn explains, between 1776 and 1810 'in most of the Chesapeake, especially in central Virginia, where half of the blacks in the region lived, slaveholding became more widespread and more deeply entrenched ... Even if Washington, Jefferson, Madison, and Monroe had devoted all their leadership skills to the single cause of black freedom, they would have failed utterly, for their society was moving inexorably in the opposite direction.'[22]

In the Lower South, yet another regional pattern became consolidated among blacks in the American revolutionary era. Manumissions proceeded in South Carolina in the 1780s at a much greater rate than ever before. Yet this was the state with the lowest rate of manumissions in the union. Accordingly, the free black community was small throughout South Carolina and Georgia. Two different trends emerged with regard to slavery in the Lower South in the last three decades of the eighteenth century. On the one hand, slavery became more deeply entrenched in South Carolina and Georgia as rice production continued to flourish. The invention of Eil Whitney's cotton gin on a Georgia plantation in 1793 and the potential for cotton growing in the Lower South and in backcountry areas to the west of existing states in the region ensured that slavery would not die a quick death. The loss of over 20,000 slaves from South Carolina during the revolutionary war, the continued importation of Africans, and the black majority that existed in large parts of the region also ensured that slavery would continue for the foreseeable future in South Carolina and Georgia. These trends were underpinned by a tough racial divide under which whites, in a self-protective vein, hardened their attitudes to conceive of blacks as debased creatures.

Yet the supposedly bleak outlook for blacks in the Lower South was tempered by a paradox, namely the growth of black autonomy within the slave system. With extensive white absenteeism on South Carolina's rice plantations – a parallel to slavery in the British Caribbean – leadership positions often fell into the hands of black drivers. It is not surprising that blacks, in such circumstances, gained more daily control of plantation life. One important way in which this was achieved lay in the spread of the task system across the Lower South, whereby slaves worked each day until they had completed various assigned tasks, controlling their own pace and time of work to some extent and using their spare time to pursue local trade, gather savings, and purchase small pieces of property. One should not push the notion of slave autonomy too far; clearly the legal restraints and punishments meted out to blacks in the Lower South were severe. Yet it is paradoxical that the highest degree of regional slave autonomy in the new American republic occurred in the states where slavery was expanding and becoming more deeply entrenched and racially divided.

The American Revolution and the Trades in Slaves, Convicts and Indentured Servants

The development of North American slavery in the revolutionary era, as outlined above, reveals a complex picture that includes deeper entrenchment of slavery in the Lower South, the growth of free blacks in the Upper South, the slowness of gradual emancipation in the northern states, and the compromises made over slavery in the framing and ratification of the Constitution. The gains made in black schools and churches were signs of a people defining their own cultural needs, but these institutions grew at a pitifully small rate. In looking at the relationship between the American Revolution and liberty, then, one is not dealing with a consistently upward trend towards freedom. But what of the trades in bound labour that had flourished for generations before the American Revolution? To what extent were they affected by the libertarian ideals of the era?

Aaron S. Fogleman has argued that the trades in unfree labour to the United States were affected profoundly by the revolution. On the eve of independence, all three trades in convicts, slaves and indentured servants were operative. By the turn of the nineteenth century they had all virtually ceased to exist. In their place, free immigration rose, setting the pattern for virtually all future arrivals to the United States. He attributes this transformation to the egalitarian spirit of the revolution: 'many Americans concluded that a large immigration of slaves, convicts, and servants was incompatible with the egalitarian ideas of the Revolution and with the cultural changes occurring in the United States. These developments transformed an immigration primarily of slaves, convicts, and indentured servants into one of free subjects.' In other parts of Fogleman's discussion, references occur to the 'egalitarian ideology' and the 'ideas of the Revolution' and their impact on these three trades.[23]

Historians have long known that the bulk of immigration to the thirteen British colonies in North America included a large unfree component and that the post-revolutionary war immigration comprised predominantly free passengers. Fogleman's explanation for these changes, however, needs qualification. The convict trade to North America, as he points out, came to an end in 1775 with the outbreak of hostilities between the British and American forces. The British then turned to keeping convicted felons in gaols or on wooden hulks on the River Thames; and while there was an unsuccessful attempt to smuggle some transported felons from Britain to the United States in 1783, the future of penal transportation from Britain lay in exiling them to Australia. Clearly, the War of Independence was decisive as an event in stopping the shipment of felons to Virginia and Maryland, but it is difficult to see how this reflected the 'egalitarian ideology' of the revolution. The trade was simply cut off because the American colonies were lost to Britain through war.

Indentured servitude was more likely to be affected by the way in which the American Revolution helped to undermine, though not extinguish, patterns of deference and subordination in the hierarchy of social groups, but it was an institution already in decline before the revolution. The disruptive effects of the War of Independence appear to have played little part in stemming the flow of indentured servants thereafter. More important was a diminished demand for bound labour in states such as Pennsylvania, with free wage labour as the preferred choice, a situation based on the economic calculation of the prices paid for each type of labour in relation to perceived productivity over time; a need for more flexible labour arrangements in the immediate post-revolutionary period, when local economies were saddled with debt and inflation during the Confederation period; and the impact of two British parliamentary Acts, passed in the 1780s, that stemmed the flow of indentured servants from Britain and Ireland. Notions of freedom may have played some part in curtailing the tide in indentured servant migrants, but they were only one among several factors and perhaps not the major factor.

The situation with the slave trade is similarly more complex than being an institution that declined because of the libertarian ideals of the

American Revolution. Certainly, individual states banned the importation of slaves in the revolutionary era. Virginia and Maryland stopped the importation of slaves in 1778 and 1783 respectively. By early 1787 only three states – Georgia, South Carolina and North Carolina – still allowed slave imports. In March 1787 South Carolina's legislature passed an Act prohibiting the importation of slaves for three years. It passed similar legislation in 1788, 1792, 1794, 1796, 1800 and 1802. The reasons why individual states took these actions were more connected to their own internal economic affairs than to altruistic motives, or a desire to promote freedom. Thus, for instance, Virginia's ban on the foreign slave trade emanated from its fear that, with a burgeoning slave population in the state undergoing rapid demographic growth, the value of slaves already living in the Old Dominion would plummet with the arrival of a surplus of newly enslaved Africans. South Carolina's 1787 prohibition on slave imports was supported by influential Lowcountry planters concerned about poor economic conditions in the state. At the Constitutional Convention in the summer of 1787 the issue of the foreign slave trade was divisive. Moreover, the clause in the Federal Constitution specifying that Congress could not interfere with the slave trade before 1808 caused disagreement during the ratification process about the extent to which Congress could or would legislate against trafficking in Africans in 1808.

The rise of an 'egalitarian ideology' may have played some part in the decline of the trades in convicts, servants and slaves in the revolutionary era. But exactly what part it played is difficult to pin down. It could be argued, in any case, that the libertarian creed of the American Revolution has been exaggerated. Little was done to improve the lot of groups such as women and Indians in the revolutionary era; though some progress was made over slavery, it was slow and protracted; and even popular sovereignty, heralded by Americans as a hallmark of their political culture, was limited in practice. The notion of the libertarian creed of the revolution is often tied up with the idea of American exceptionalism. In Fogleman's account, it almost plays the part of something that was America's destiny. In recent years, the acceptance of American exceptionalism has come under greater scrutiny. In looking at the trades in unfree labour to revolutionary America, the evidence cited above shows a more complex situation at work, with supply factors and the internal economic needs of American states playing a more important role than ideas fostered by the American Revolution.

By 1800 considerable progress had been made towards ensuring that future immigration to the United States would be a diaspora of free migrants. The bonded labour that was so prevalent in the seventeenth and eighteenth centuries had largely ceased to fill an economic function. The problem of slavery had also attracted the attention of some of the finest men of the revolutionary generation and had been addressed in some of the founding documents of the United States. But America entered the nineteenth century with slavery expanding throughout the South, with racial lines becoming more hardened in the southern states, and with a slow, gradual approach to abolitionism in the northern states. Black communities in the North were beginning to develop a strong sense of identity, establishing schools and churches to reflect pride in their own endeavours. In the Lower South slave autonomy was notable on plantations despite the rigours of the work regimen. And yet the gains made by blacks were met, step by step, by frustration, delays and equivocation on the part of the white populace. In short, slavery cast a dark spectre over the American nation as Jefferson took up the presidency and it was not to end until the bloodiest war on American soil had nearly torn the nation asunder.

Notes

1. Samuel Johnson, *Taxation No Tyranny, An Answer to the Resolutions and Addresses of the American Congress* (London, 1774), p. 89.
2. Thomas Hutchinson, *Strictures upon the Declaration of the Congress at Philadelphia* (London, 1776), pp. 9–10.
3. *A Serious Address to the Rulers of America, on the Inconsistency of Their Conduct Respecting Slavery* ... (Trenton, 1783), pp. 12–13.
4. Edmund S. Morgan, 'Slavery and Freedom: The American Paradox', *Journal of American History*, 59 (1972), pp. 5–29, reprinted in his book *The Challenge of the American Revolution* (New York: W. W. Norton, 1976), ch. 3.
5. Quoted in Sylvia R. Frey, *Water from the Rock: Black Resistance in a Revolutionary Age* (Princeton: Princeton University Press, 1991), p. 78.
6. George Washington to John Francis Mercer, 5 Dec. 1786, in W. W. Abbot et al. (eds), *The Papers of George Washington: Confederation Series*, 6 vols (Charlottesville, VA: University of Virginia Press, 1995), iv, p. 442.
7. George Washington to John Francis Mercer, 9 Sept. 1786, ibid., iv, p. 243.
8. Quoted in John P. Kaminski (ed.), *A Necessary Evil? Slavery and the Debate over the Constitution* (Madison, WI: Madison House, 1995), p. 244.
9. Quoted in ibid., p. 277.
10. James Madison to Joseph Jones, 28 Nov. 1780, in William T. Hutchinson and William M. E. Rachal (eds), *The Papers of James Madison* (Chicago: University of Chicago Press, 1962), ii, p. 209.

11. 'Memorandum on an African Colony for Freed Slaves,' c. 20 Oct. 1789 (in Madison's hand) in Charles F. Hobson and Robert A. Rutland (eds), *The Papers of James Madison* (Charlottesville, VA: University Press of Virginia, 1979), xii, pp. 437–8.

12. William W. Freehling, 'The Founding Fathers, Conditional Antislavery, and the Nonradicalism of the American Revolution' in his *The Reintegration of American History: Slavery and the Civil War* (New York: Oxford University Press, 1994), ch. 2.

13. William Peden (ed.), Thomas Jefferson, *Notes on the State of Virginia* (Chapel Hill: University of North Carolina Press, 1955), p. 138.

14. Thomas Jefferson to Thomas Cooper, 10 Sept. 1814, in Andrew A. Lipscomb and Albert Ellery Bergh (eds), *The Writings of Thomas Jefferson*, 20 vols (Washington, DC, 1903–4), xiv, p. 183.

15. Thomas Jefferson to John Holmes, 22 Apr. 1820, in Paul Leicester Ford (ed.), *The Works of Thomas Jefferson*, 12 vols (New York, 1904–5), x, p. 157.

16. Joseph J. Ellis and Eric S. Lander in *Nature*, 5 Nov. 1998.

17. Staughton Lynd, 'The Compromise of 1787', *Political Science Quarterly*, 81 (1966), pp. 225–50.

18. *Maryland Gazette*, 18 Jan. 1788, quoted in Kaminski (ed.), *A Necessary Evil?*, p. 173.

19. Thomas B. Wait to George Thatcher, 8 Jan. 1788, ibid., p. 79.

20. *The Federalist*, no. 54, 12 Feb. 1788, ibid., p. 144.

21. Quoted in Kaminski (ed.), *A Necessary Evil?*, p. 56.

22. Richard S. Dunn, 'Black Society in the Chesapeake, 1776–1810' in Ira Berlin and Ronald Hoffman (eds), *Slavery and Freedom in the Age of the American Revolution* (Charlottesville, VA: University Press of Virginia, 1983), p. 81.

23. Aaron S. Fogleman, 'From Slaves, Convicts, and Servants to Free Passengers: The Transformation of Immigration in the Era of the American Revolution', *Journal of American History*, 85 (1998), p. 45.

Bibliography

The first two centuries of slavery and servitude in North America have long attracted historical attention, but the literature on these aspects of labour has burgeoned over the past generation. Brief overviews can be found in Philip D. Morgan, 'African Migration' and Sharon V. Salinger, 'Labor: Colonial Times through 1820' in Mary K. Cayton, Elliot J. Gorn and Peter W. Williams (eds), *Encyclopedia of American Social History*, 3 vols (New York: Scribner, 1993), ii, pp. 795–809, 1433–45. Helpful surveys of early North American slavery can be found in three articles: Peter H. Wood, '"I Did the Best I Could for My Day": The Study of Early Black History during the Second Reconstruction, 1960 to 1976', *William and Mary Quarterly*, 3rd series (hereafter cited as *WMQ*), 35 (1978), pp. 185–225; Ira Berlin, 'Time, Space, and the Evolution of Afro-American Society on British Mainland North America', *American Historical Review* (hereafter cited as *AHR*), 85 (1980), pp. 44–78; and Jon F. Sensbach, 'Charting a Course in Early African-American History', *WMQ*, 50 (1993), pp. 394–405. Berlin's article has been expanded into a book, which is currently the most up-to-date synthesis of work on early North American slavery: *Many Thousands Gone: The First Two Centuries of Slavery in North America* (Cambridge, MA: Harvard University Press, 1998).

Relevant material on slavery and servitude in early North America also appears in Winthrop D. Jordan, *White over Black: American Attitudes toward the Negro, 1550–1812* (Chapel Hill: University of North Carolina Press, 1968); John J. McCusker and Russell R. Menard, *The Economy of British America, 1607–1789* (Chapel Hill: University of North Carolina Press, 1985); Jack P. Greene, *Pursuits of Happiness: The Social Development of Early Modern British Colonies and the Formation of American Culture* (Chapel Hill: University of North Carolina Press, 1988); Nicholas Canny (ed.), *The Oxford History of the British Empire: Volume 1: The Origins of Empire: British Overseas Enterprise to the Close of the Seventeenth Century* (Oxford: Oxford University Press, 1998); P. J. Marshall (ed.), *The Oxford History of the British Empire: Volume II:*

The Eighteenth Century (Oxford: Oxford University Press, 1998); and Stanley L. Engerman and Robert E. Gallman (eds), *The Cambridge Economic History of the United States: Volume I: The Colonial Era* (New York: Cambridge University Press, 1996).

Any study of slavery in the New World requires a background knowledge of slavery in the Old World. On this subject some helpful publications are David Brion Davis's landmark book *The Problem of Slavery in Western Culture* (Ithaca, NY: Cornell University Press, 1966); Barbara L. Solow, 'Slavery and Colonization' and William D. Phillips, Jr, 'The Old World Background of Slavery in the Americas', both in Solow (ed.), *Slavery and the Rise of the Atlantic System* (Cambridge: Cambridge University Press, 1991), pp. 21–61; and Robin Blackburn, *The Making of New World Slavery: From the Baroque to the Modern, 1492–1800* (London: Verso, 1997). The Atlantic slave trade has attracted innumerable studies. Philip D. Curtin's *The Atlantic Slave Trade: A Census* (Madison, WI: University of Wisconsin Press, 1969) is a reference work of continuing importance, now in need of a second edition. Recent studies include Herbert S. Klein, *The Atlantic Slave Trade* (New York: Cambridge University Press, 1999) and David Eltis, *The Rise of African Slavery in the Americas* (New York: Cambridge University Press, 2000). A textbook overview of colonial North American slavery appears in Peter Kolchin, *American Slavery* (New York: HarperCollins, 1993), chs 1 and 2.

The broad context of indentured servitude lay in the migration of British, Irish and German emigrants to North America between the founding of Jamestown and the first shots fired at Concord. The broad contours of this diaspora are outlined in Bernard Bailyn, *The Peopling of British North America: An Introduction* (New York: Alfred A. Knopf, 1986) and Nicholas Canny (ed.), *Europeans on the Move: Studies on European Migration, 1500–1800* (Oxford: Oxford University Press, 1994). Interesting articles dealing with the labour problem in North America in the seventeenth and eighteenth centuries include Marcus Rediker, '"Good Hands, Stout Heart, and Fast Feet": The History and Culture of Working People in Early America', *Labour/Le Travailleur*, 10 (1982), pp. 123–44; Richard S. Dunn, 'Servants and Slaves: The Recruitment and Employment of Labor' in Jack P. Greene and J. R. Pole (eds), *Colonial British America: Essays in the New History of the Early Modern Era* (Baltimore: Johns Hopkins University Press, 1984), pp. 157–94; and Hermann Wellenreuther, 'Labor in the Era of the

American Revolution: A Discussion of Recent Concepts and Theories', *Labor History*, 22 (1981), pp. 573–600. For the argument that the egalitarianism of the American Revolution transformed enforced migration to North America, see Aaron S. Fogleman, 'From Slaves, Convicts, and Servants to Free Passengers: The Transformation of Immigration in the Era of the American Revolution,' *Journal of American History* (hereafter *JAH*), 85 (1998), pp. 43–76.

Chapter 1 Indentured Servitude in the Seventeenth Century

Older studies still contain some useful material on indentured servitude during the seventeenth century. Particularly useful are Richard B. Morris, *Government and Labor in Early America* (New York: Columbia University Press, 1946) and Abbot Emerson Smith, *Colonists in Bondage: White Servitude and Convict Labor in America, 1607–1776* (Chapel Hill: University of North Carolina Press, 1947). Brief but stimulating modern overviews of the topic include Dunn, 'Servants and Slaves'; McCusker and Menard, *Economy of British America*, ch. 11; Edmund S. Morgan, *American Slavery, American Freedom: The Ordeal of Colonial Virginia* (New York: W. W. Norton, 1975); David Souden, 'English Indentured Servants and the Transatlantic Colonial Economy' in Shula Marks and Peter Richardson (eds), *International Labour Migration: Historical Perspectives* (London: Temple Smith, 1984), pp. 19–33; Henry A. Gemery, 'Markets for Migrants: English indentured servitude and emigration in the seventeenth and eighteenth centuries' in P. C. Emmer (ed.), *Colonialism and Migration: Indentured Labour before and after Slavery* (Dordrecht: Martinus Nijhoff, 1986), pp. 33–54; K. G. Davies, *The North Atlantic World in the Seventeenth Century: Europe and the World in the Age of Expansion* (Minneapolis, MN: University of Minnesota Press, 1974); and David W. Galenson, 'The Rise and Fall of Indentured Servitude in the Americas: An Economic Analysis', *Journal of Economic History* (hereafter *JEcH*), 44 (1984), pp. 1–26.

Indentured servitude was an institution that stemmed from the practice of hired labour in pre-industrial England. Essential background on these young male and female workers who lived and worked in their masters' households on annual contracts can be found in Ann Kussmaul, *Servants in Husbandry in Early Modern England* (Cambridge: Cambridge University Press, 1981). Comparison of servant labour in England and its North American colonies is included in Robert J. Steinfeld, *The Invention of Free Labor: The Employment Relation in*

English and American Law and Culture, 1350–1870 (Chapel Hill: University of North Carolina Press, 1991), esp. pp. 15–54. The most substantial modern text dealing with indentured servants is David W. Galenson, *White Servitude in Colonial America: An Economic Analysis* (Cambridge: Cambridge University Press, 1981). Based on an analysis of the surviving servant registers for Bristol, Middlesex and London, this book offers a sophisticated treatment of the age and sex distribution of the servant population, of their occupations and literacy, and of their role in the North American labour market. For the general significance of servitude for the history of the Chesapeake, see Greene, *Pursuits of Happiness*. The overall context of emigration to Virginia and Maryland is covered in Russell R. Menard, 'British Migration to the Chesapeake Colonies in the Seventeenth Century' in Lois Green Carr, Philip D. Morgan and Jean B. Russo (eds), *Colonial Chesapeake Society* (Chapel Hill: University of North Carolina Press, 1988), pp. 99–132.

The class composition of the indentured servants has attracted debate between Galenson and Mildred Campbell, who had published a pioneer account based on some of the registration lists in 'Social Origins of Some Early Americans' in James Morton Smith (ed.), *Seventeenth-Century America: Essays in Colonial History* (Chapel Hill: University of North Carolina Press, 1959), pp. 63–89. The exchange can be followed in Galenson, '"Middling People" or "Common Sort"? The Social Origins of Some Early Americans Reexamined', with a response by Campbell in the *WMQ*, 35 (1978), pp. 499–540, and in Galenson's 'The Social Origins of Some Early Americans: Rejoinder', with a reply by Campbell in *WMQ*, 36 (1979), pp. 264–86. The debate centred on the overall representativeness of information in the registration lists pertaining to the social class of indentured emigrants.

Particular discussion has centred on the largest surviving indentured servant list for the seventeenth century, kept at Bristol between 1654 and 1686. Apart from the discussion in Galenson's *White Servitude*, the following studies also concentrate on the interpretation of this document: James Horn, 'Servant Emigration to the Chesapeake in the Seventeenth Century' in Thad W. Tate and David L. Ammerman (eds), *The Chesapeake in the Seventeenth Century: Essays on Anglo-American Society* (Chapel Hill: University of North Carolina Press, 1979), pp. 51–95; David Souden, 'Rogues, Whores and Vagabonds? Indentured Servant Emigrants to North America, and the Case of Mid-Seventeenth Century Bristol', *Social History*, 3 (1978), pp. 23–41; and

David Harris Sacks, *The Widening Gate: Bristol and the Atlantic Economy, 1450–1700* (Berkeley, CA: University of California Press, 1991), ch. 9. Horn has expanded his work into a carefully nuanced comparative study entitled *Adapting to a New World: English Society in the Seventeenth-Century Chesapeake* (Chapel Hill: University of North Carolina Press, 1994).

Despite the fine work outlined above, there is no fully comprehensive appraisal of servitude in early North America. The voice of the indentured servant is often lacking owing to the paucity of written evidence from such lower-class people. An exception can be found in T. H. Breen, James H. Lewis and Keith Schlesinger, 'Motive for Murder: A Servant's Life in Virginia, 1678', *WMQ*, 40 (1983), pp. 106–20. One detailed study of the life of someone who emerged successfully out of servitude in Maryland is Lois Green Carr, 'Daniel Clocker's Adventure: From Servant to Freeholder' in Ian K. Steele and Nancy L. Rhoden (eds), *The Human Tradition in Colonial America* (Wilmington, DE: Scholarly Resources, Inc., 1999), pp. 97–118. The fate of indentured servants after their term was up has failed to attract much analysis. For some interesting case studies, however, see Russell R. Menard, 'From Servant to Freeholder: Status Mobility and Property Accumulation in Seventeenth-Century Maryland', *WMQ*, 30 (1973), pp. 37–64; Lorena S. Walsh, 'Servitude and Opportunity in Charles County, Maryland, 1658–1705' in Aubrey C. Land, Lois Green Carr and Edward C. Papenfuse (eds), *Law, Society and Politics in Early Maryland* (Baltimore, MD: Johns Hopkins University Press, 1977), pp. 111–33; and Lois Green Carr and Russell R. Menard, 'Immigration and Opportunity: The Freedman in Early Colonial Maryland' in Tate and Ammerman (eds), *Chesapeake in the Seventeenth Century*, pp. 206–42. Carr has synthesized material on the life expectations of seventeenth-century servants in 'Emigration and the Standard of Living: The Seventeenth-Century Chesapeake', *JEcH*, 52 (1992), pp. 271–91.

Chapter 2 From Servitude to Slavery

The transition from servitude to slavery in the southern American colonies is best approached through consideration of the potential available labour force that could be deployed on plantations. The triracial nature of early North American society provides a framework for discussion. The failure to harness Native Americans to plantation agriculture is explained in books such as Davies, *North Atlantic World*;

C. Duncan Rice, *The Rise and Fall of Black Slavery* (Baton Rouge: Louisiana State University Press, 1975), ch. 3; Wesley Frank Craven, *White, Red, and Black: The Seventeenth-Century Virginian* (Charlottesville, VA: University Press of Virginia, 1971); and Gary B. Nash, *Red, White and Black: The Peoples of Early America*, 3rd edn (Englewood Cliffs, NJ: Prentice Hall, 1992). A useful overview is provided in Peter C. Mancall, 'Native Americans and Europeans in English America, 1500–1700' in Canny (ed.), *The Oxford History of the British Empire: vol. 1*, pp. 328–50. Further analysis of the triracial groups that made up early American society is available in T. H. Breen and Stephen Innes, *'Myne Own Ground': Race and Freedom on Virginia's Eastern Shore, 1640–1676* (New York: Oxford University Press, 1980); J. Douglas Deal, *Race and Class in Colonial Virginia: Indians, Englishmen, and Africans on the Eastern Shore during the Seventeenth Century* (New York: Garland, 1993); and Timothy Silver, *A New Face on the Countryside: Indians, Colonists, and Slaves in South Atlantic Forests, 1500–1800* (Cambridge: Cambridge University Press, 1990). A recent study that adds to these discussions is Betty Wood, *The Origins of American Slavery: Freedom and Bondage in the English Colonies* (New York: Hill and Wang, 1997). James Axtell's essay 'Colonial America without the Indians', reprinted in his *After Columbus: Essays in the Ethnohistory of Colonial North America* (New York: Oxford University Press, 1988), ch. 11, has some interesting speculations on the relationship between Native Americans and the emergence of slavery in the seventeenth-century Chesapeake.

Considerable debate has focused on whether the first blacks imported into Virginia in 1619 were initially treated as servants and only reduced after 1660 to the status of slaves. An influential argument that such a situation pertained was published in Oscar and Mary F. Handlin, 'Origins of the Southern Labor System', *WMQ*, 7 (1950), pp. 199–222. In *White over Black*, Winthrop Jordan presented a different case: that little evidence exists for the Chesapeake to show how blacks were treated between 1619 and 1640, but that mounting evidence shows that between 1640 and 1660 some blacks were being treated as slaves. Jordan also argued that racism accompanied these changes in the treatment and status of blacks in the seventeenth-century Chesapeake. Further material on the status of blacks in Virginia around the middle of the seventeenth century is included in Carl N. Degler, 'Slavery and the Genesis of American Race Prejudice', *Comparative Studies in Society and*

History, 2 (1959), pp. 49–66; Paul C. Palmer, 'Servant into Slave: The Evolution of the Legal Status of the Negro Labourer in Colonial Virginia', *South Atlantic Quarterly*, 65 (1966, pp. 355–70); Robert McColley, 'Slavery in Virginia, 1619–1660: A Reexamination' in Robert H. Abzug and Stephen E. Maizlish (eds), *New Perspectives on Race and Slavery in America: Essays in Honor of Kenneth M. Stampp* (Lexington: University Press of Kentucky, 1986); Alden T. Vaughan, *Roots of American Racism: Essays on the Colonial Experience* (New York: Oxford University Press, 1995); and Kathleen M. Brown, *Good Wives, Nasty Wenches, and Anxious Patriarchs: Gender, Race, and Power in Colonial Virginia* (Chapel Hill: University of North Carolina Press, 1996).

The transition from indentured servitude to slavery in Virginia has been explored from various perspectives. Emphasis on changing labour relations, based on race and class differences, along with the impact of Bacon's Rebellion of 1676 on the white propertied classes, is emphasized in T. H. Breen, 'A Changing Labor Force and Race Relations in Virginia, 1660–1710' in his *Puritans and Adventurers: Change and Persistence in Early America* (New York: Oxford University Press, 1980) and in Morgan, *American Slavery, American Freedom*, ch. 13. Economic historians have contributed valuably to this subject in a number of studies: Allan Kulikoff, *Tobacco and Slaves: The Development of Southern Cultures in the Chesapeake, 1680–1800* (Chapel Hill: University of North Carolina Press, 1986); Russell R. Menard, 'From Servants to Slaves: The Transformation of the Chesapeake Labor System', *Southern Studies*, 16 (1977), pp. 355–90; Galenson, *White Servitude*, pp. 141–9; and David W. Galenson, 'Economic Aspects of the Growth of Slavery in the Seventeenth-Century Chesapeake', in Solow (ed.), *Slavery and the Rise of the Atlantic System*, ch. 11.

The shift from servitude to slavery in the South Carolina Lowcountry has not attracted such detailed study, but helpful material is available in Peter H. Wood, *Black Majority: Negroes in Colonial South Carolina from 1670 through the Stono Rebellion* (New York: Alfred A. Knopf, 1974); Daniel C. Littlefield, *Rice and Slaves: Ethnicity and the Slave Trade in Colonial South Carolina* (Urbana-Champaign, IL: University of Illinois Press, 1981); Aaron M. Shatzman, *Servants into Planters: The Origin of an American Image: Land Acquisition and Status Mobility in Seventeenth-Century South Carolina* (New York: Garland, 1989); Philip D. Morgan, *Slave Counterpoint: Black Culture in the Eighteenth-Century Chesapeake and Lowcountry* (Chapel Hill: University of North Carolina Press, 1998);

and Russell R. Menard, 'The Africanization of the Lowcountry Labor Force' in Winthrop D. Jordan and Sheila L. Skemp (eds), *Race and Family in the Colonial South* (Jackson, MS: University of Mississippi Press, 1987), pp. 81–108. The changing nature of servitude in Georgia is explored in Ralph Gray and Betty Wood, 'The Transition from Indentured to Involuntary Servitude in Colonial Georgia', *Explorations in Economic History*, 13 (1976), pp. 353–70.

Chapter 3 Convicts, Indentured Servants and Redemptioners, 1680–1775

Until comparatively recently, study of convicts and indentured servants in eighteenth-century North America relied largely on two older studies: Morris's *Government and Labor in Early America* and Smith's *Colonists in Bondage*. But like other aspects of social history linked to lower-class experience, a number of modern studies have transformed our understanding of these groups. Richard Hoftstadter had some intelligent observations on both groups in his book *America at 1750: A Social Portrait* (New York: Alfred A. Knopf, 1972), the first part of an incomplete multivolume history of American social history. Further investigation of both convicts and indentured servants can be found in Bernard Bailyn, *Voyagers to the West: Emigration from Britain to America on the Eve of the Revolution* (New York: Alfred A. Knopf, 1986), the first detailed instalment of an ambitious project devoted to the peopling of the Americas in the early modern era. Bailyn has good sections on the market for indentured servants and convicts in the Chesapeake just prior to the American Revolution. This volume includes modern colour portraits of these groups, based on details given in runaway advertisements in newspapers. Descriptive material on convicts, indentured servants and redemptioners is contained in Stephanie Grauman Wolf, *As Various as their Land: The Everyday Lives of Eighteenth-Century Americans* (New York: HarperCollins, 1994).

Older studies of indentured servitude include Eugene I. McCormac, *White Servitude in Maryland, 1634–1820* (Baltimore: Johns Hopkins University Press, 1904); James C. Ballagh, *White Servitude in the Colony of Virginia: A Study of the System of Indentured Labor in the American Colonies* (Baltimore, MD: Johns Hopkins University Press, 1895); John Spencer Bassett, *Slavery and Servitude in the Colony of North Carolina* (Baltimore, MD: Johns Hopkins University Press, 1896); Karl Frederick

Geiser, *Redemptioners and Indentured Servants in the Colony and Commonwealth of Pennsylvania* (New Haven: Yale University Press, 1901);
and Cheesman A. Herrick, *White Servitude in Pennsylvania: Indentured
and Redemption Labor in Colony and Commonwealth* (Philadelphia, PA:
J. J. McVey, 1926). But these books have largely been supplanted by the
works cited below.

General studies of eighteenth-century indentured servants include
Galenson, *White Servitude* and his 'British Servants and the Colonial
Indenture System in the Eighteenth Century', *Journal of Southern
History*, 44 (1978), pp. 59–66; Dunn, 'Servants and Slaves'; and a
review essay by Sharon V. Salinger entitled 'Labor, Markets, and
Opportunity: Indentured Servitude in Early America', *Labor History*,
38 (1997), pp. 311–38. The latter has attracted a fierce riposte in Farley
Grubb's communication 'Labor, Markets, and Opportunity: Indentured
Servitude in Early America, a Rejoinder to Salinger', *Labor History*, 39
(1998), pp. 235–41. On the supply of indentured servants, see John
Wareing, 'Migration to London and Transatlantic Emigration of Indentured Servants, 1683–1775', *Journal of Historical Geography*, 7 (1981),
pp. 356–78. Lois Green Carr has recently attempted to evaluate the
servant experience in 'Emigration and the Standard of Living: The
Eighteenth-Century Chesapeake' in John J. McCusker and Kenneth
Morgan (eds), *The Early Modern Atlantic Economy* (Cambridge: Cambridge University Press, 2000).

The urban dimension of servitude in relation to other forms of
labour is analyzed in Gary B. Nash, *The Urban Crucible: Social Change,
Political Consciousness, and the Origins of the American Revolution*
(Cambridge, MA: Harvard University Press, 1979). Irish servant migra-
tion is covered in R. J. Dickson, *Ulster Emigration to Colonial America,
1718–1783* (London: Routledge and Kegan Paul, 1966); Marianne S.
Wokeck, *Trade in Strangers: The Beginnings of Mass Migration to North
America* (University Park, PA: Pennsylvania State University Press,
1999); L. M. Cullen, 'The Irish Diaspora of the Seventeenth and
Eighteenth Centuries' in Canny (ed.), *Europeans on the Move*, pp. 113–
49; Maldwyn A. Jones, 'The Scotch-Irish in British America' in Bernard
Bailyn and Philip D. Morgan (eds), *Strangers within the Realm: Cultural
Margins of the First British Empire* (Chapel Hill: University of North
Carolina Press, 1991), pp. 284–313; Audrey Lockhart, *Some Aspects
of Emigration from Ireland to the North American Colonies between 1660
and 1775* (New York: Arno Press, 1976); and Thomas M. Truxes,

Irish-American Trade, 1660–1783 (New York: Cambridge University Press, 1988), ch. 7.

The main regional study of eighteenth-century indentured servants is Sharon V. Salinger's *'To Serve Well and Faithfully': Labor and Indentured Servants in Pennsylvania, 1682–1800* (Cambridge: Cambridge University Press, 1987). This study concentrates particularly on Philadelphia. See also Robert O. Heavner, *Economic Aspects of Indentured Servitude in Colonial Philadelphia* (New York: Arno Press, 1978) and Farley Grubb, 'The Market for Indentured Servants: Evidence on the Efficiency of Forward Labor Contracting in Philadelphia, 1745–1773', *JEcH*, 45 (1985), pp. 855–68, and 'Servant Auction Records and Immigration into the Delaware Valley, 1745–1831: The Proportion of Females among Immigrant Servants', *Proceedings of the American Philosophical Society*, 133 (1989, pp. 154–69).

Material on indentured servitude in other colonies is rather thin. Some useful material, however, appears in Margaret M. R. Kellow, 'Indentured Servitude in Eighteenth-Century Maryland', *Histoire Sociale/Social History*, 17 (1984), pp. 229–55, and Warren B. Smith, *White Servitude in Colonial South Carolina* (Columbia, SC: University of South Carolina Press, 1961). Two detailed contemporary accounts of indentured servants are available in modern editions: Edward M. Riley (ed.), *The Journal of John Harrower* (Williamsburg, VA: Holt, Rinehart and Winston, 1963) and Susan E. Klepp and Billy G. Smith (eds), *The Infortunate: The Voyage and Adventures of William Moraley, an Indentured Servant* (University Park, PA: Pennsylvania State University Press, 1992). The decline of indentured servitude in North America is treated in William Miller, 'The Effects of the American Revolution on Indentured Servitude', *Pennsylvania History*, 7 (1940), pp. 131–41; Charlotte Erickson, 'Why did Contract Labour not work in the Nineteenth-Century United States?' in Marks and Richardson (eds), *International Labour Migration*, pp. 34–56; and Grubb, 'The End of European Immigrant Servitude in the United States: An Economic Analysis of Market Collapse, 1772–1835', *JEcH*, 54 (1994), pp. 794–824.

In recent years, convict transportees to colonial North America have informed several independent analyses. The most up-to-date, book-length treatment of this group appears in A. Roger Ekirch, *Bound for America: The Transportation of British Convicts to the Colonies, 1718–1775* (Oxford: Oxford University Press, 1987). The ambivalent attitudes expressed by both British and American commentators on transportation are only addressed tangentially in Ekirch's book; a fuller discussion appears in Kenneth Morgan, 'English and American Attitudes towards Convict Transportation, 1718–1775', *History*, 72 (1987), pp. 416–31. The labour market for convicts in the late colonial Chesapeake is covered in Smith, *Colonists in Bondage*; Bailyn, *Voyagers to the West*; F. H. Schmidt, 'Sold and Driven: Assignment of Convicts in Eighteenth-Century Virginia', *Push from the Bush: A Bulletin of Social History*, 23 (1986), pp. 2–27; Kenneth Morgan, 'The Organization of the Convict Trade to Maryland: Stevenson, Randolph & Cheston, 1768–1775', *WMQ*, 42 (1985), pp. 201–27; and Farley Grubb, 'The Transatlantic Market for British Convict Labor', *JEcH*, 60 (2000, pp. 94–122).

Essential background material on convicts is provided in J. M. Beattie, *Crime and the Courts in England, 1660–1800* (Princeton, NJ: Princeton University Press, 1986). For felons transported from northeast England, see the discussion in Gwenda Morgan and Peter Rushton, *Rogues, Thieves and the Rule of Law: The Problem of Law Enforcement in North-East England, 1718–1800* (London: UCL Press, 1998), ch. 7. Two additional useful studies on transported convicts to the American colonies are Alan Atkinson, 'The Free-born Englishman Transported: Convict Rights as a Measure of Eighteenth-Century Empire', *Past and Present*, no. 144 (1994), pp. 88–115, and Kenneth Morgan, 'The Nature of Convict Transportation to North America, 1718–1775' in Clare Anderson (ed.), *Colonial Places, Convict Spaces: Penal Transportation in Global Context c. 1600–1940* (Basingstoke: Macmillan, 2001). Peter Wilson Coldham's *Emigrants in Chains: A Social History of Forced Emigration to the Americas 1607–1776* (Stroud: Alan Sutton, 1992), though incorporating primary research, adds nothing interpretatively to these accounts.

A handful of scholars have concentrated their research on the German redemptioner migrants of the eighteenth century. Wokeck's preliminary conclusions, published in articles, have now been incorporated into her *Trade in Strangers*. The economic aspects of the redemptioner system are analyzed in several articles by Grubb: 'Morbidity and Mortality on the North Atlantic Passage: Eighteenth-Century German Immigration', *Journal of Interdisciplinary History* (hereafter *JIH*), 17 (1987), pp. 565–85; 'Redemptioner Immigration to Pennsylvania: Evidence on Contract Choice and Profitability', *JEcH*, 46 (1986), pp. 407–18; 'German Immigration to Pennsylvania, 1709–1820', *JIH*, 20 (1990), pp. 417–36; and 'The Auction of Redemptioner Servants, Philadelphia, 1771–1804: An

Economic Analysis', *JEcH*, 48 (1988), pp. 583–603. A recent detailed study of the German diaspora to colonial North America is Aaron Spencer Fogleman's *Hopeful Journeys: German Immigration, Settlement, and Political Culture in Colonial America, 1717–1775* (Philadelphia, PA: University of Pennsylvania Press, 1996). Tracing the Palatine migrants from their origins to their places of settlement in the colonies, Fogleman concentrates on the adjustments made by these people to their new environment. He argues that the migrants became Americanized but also retained important traits from their German background. Other helpful studies of German migrants in the colonies are Gunther Moltmann, 'The Migration of German Redemptioners to North America, 1720–1820' in Emmer (ed.), *Colonialism and Migration*; A. G. Roeber, *Palatines, Liberty, and Property: German Lutherans in Colonial America* (Baltimore, MD: Johns Hopkins University Press, 1993); and Mark Häberlein, 'German Migrants in Colonial Pennsylvania: Resources, Opportunities, and Experience', *WMQ*, 50 (1993), pp. 555–74. The decline of the redemptioner system in North America is the theme of Hans-Jürgen Grabbe, 'Das Ende des Redemptioner-System in den Vereinigten Staaten', *Amerikastudien*, 29 (1984), pp. 291–6, and Grubb, 'The End of European Immigrant Servitude'. The best-known contemporary account of German redemptioner migration has been translated into English in Oscar Handlin and John Clive (eds), *Gottlieb Mittelberger's Journey to Pennsylvania in the Year 1750 and Return to Germany in the Year 1754* (Cambridge, MA: Harvard University Press, 1960).

Chapter 4 Slavery in the Eighteenth Century

Overviews of the variegated nature of slavery in eighteenth-century North America include Kolchin, *American Slavery*; Greene, *Pursuits of Happiness*; James Walvin, *Black Ivory: A History of British Slavery* (London: HarperCollins, 1992); Robert William Fogel, *Without Consent or Contract: The Rise and Fall of American Slavery* (New York: W. W. Norton, 1989); Jordan, *White over Black*; Ira Berlin and Philip D. Morgan (eds), *Cultivation and Culture: Labor and the Shaping of Slave Life in the Americas* (Charlottesville, VA: University Press of Virginia, 1993); and Blackburn, *The Making of New World Slavery*, ch. 11. The legal aspects of slavery are discussed in William M. Wiecek, 'The Statutory Law of Slavery and Race in the Thirteen Mainland Colonies of British America', *WMQ*, 34 (1977), pp. 258–80. An important theoretical position is outlined in Stefano Fenoaltea, 'Slavery and Supervision in Comparative Perspective: A Model', *JEcH*, 44 (1984), pp. 635–88. The material remains of slaves are explored in Leland Ferguson, *Uncommon Ground: Archaeology and Early African America, 1650–1800* (Washington, DC: Smithsonian Institution Press, 1992). A good example of ingenious recent research on the cultural life of slaves can be found in Shane White and Graham White, 'Slave Clothing and African-American Culture in the Eighteenth and Nineteenth Centuries', *Past and Present*, no. 148 (1995), pp. 149–86. The two major studies of the subject that have recently appeared are Berlin, *Many Thousands Gone* and Morgan's *Slave Counterpoint*. Both of these fine books are especially attuned to regional variations in slave life and work; both look at slavery in a broad, comparative way; and both emphasize the achievements of blacks in their attempts to survive in racially hostile environments.

Slavery in the Chesapeake has attracted a number of fine studies, notably *Slave Counterpoint*; Morgan, *American Slavery, American Freedom*; Kulikoff, *Tobacco and Slaves*; Gerald W. Mullin, *Flight and Rebellion: Slave Resistance in Eighteenth-Century Virginia* (New York: Oxford University Press, 1972); Mechal Sobel, *The World they made Together: Black and White Values in Eighteenth-Century Virginia* (Princeton: Princeton University Press, 1987); Lorena S. Walsh, 'Slave Life, Slave Society, and Tobacco Production in the Tidewater Chesapeake, 1620–1820' in Berlin and Morgan (eds), *Cultivation and Culture*; Jean Butenhoff Lee, 'The Problem of Slave Community in the Eighteenth-Century Chesapeake', *WMQ*, 43 (1986), pp. 333–61; Carole Shammas, 'Black Women's Work and the Evolution of Plantation Society in Virginia', *Labor History*, 26 (1985), pp. 5–28; and Lorena S. Walsh, *From Calabar to Carter's Grove: The History of a Virginia Slave Community* (Charlottesville, VA: University Press of Virginia, 1997). For North Carolina, the best studies are Marvin L. Michael Kay and Lorin Lee Cary, *Slavery in North Carolina, 1748–1775* (Chapel Hill: University of North Carolina Press, 1995) and Jon F. Sensbach, *A Separate Canaan: The Making of an Afro-Moravian World in North Carolina, 1763–1840* (Chapel Hill: University of North Carolina Press, 1998).

For the Lower South, the main studies of slavery are Wood, *Black Majority*; Littlefield, *Rice and Slaves*; Morgan, *Slave Counterpoint*; Robert Olwell, *Masters, Slaves, and Subjects: The Culture of Power in the South Carolina Lowcountry 1740–1790* (Ithaca, NY: Cornell University Press, 1998); M. Eugene Sirmans, 'The Legal Status of the Slave in South Carolina, 1670–1740', *Journal of Southern History*, 28 (1962), pp. 462–73; Betty Wood, *Slavery in Colonial Georgia, 1730–1775* (Athens, GA: University of Georgia Press, 1984) and *Women's Work, Men's Work: The Informal Slave Economies of Lowcountry Georgia* (Athens, GA: University of Georgia Press, 1995). The problems of establishing a black creole population in the Lower South are investigated in Russell R. Menard, 'Slave Demography in the Lowcountry, 1670–1740: From Frontier Society to Plantation Regime', *South Carolina Historical Magazine*, 96 (1995), pp. 280–303. The evolution of paternalism in the Lower South is traced in Jeffrey Robert Young, *Domesticating Slavery: The Master Class in Georgia and South Carolina, 1670–1837* (Chapel Hill: University of North Carolina Press, 1999). Slavery in a westward extension of the South is probed in Daniel H. Usner, *Indians, Settlers and Slaves in a Frontier Exchange Economy: The Lower Mississippi Valley before 1783* (Chapel Hill: University of North Carolina Press, 1992).

For the northern colonies, black life, culture and work are the subject of several studies: William D. Piersen, *Black Yankees: The Development of an Afro-American Subculture in Eighteenth-Century New England* (Amherst, MA: University of Massachusetts Press, 1988); Lorenzo Johnston Greene, *The Negro in Colonial New England* (New York: Columbia University Press, 1942, repr. 1968); Edgar J. McManus, *Black Bondage in the North* (Syracuse, NY: Syracuse University Press, 1973); Gary B. Nash, *Race, Class, and Politics: Essays on American Colonial and Revolutionary Society* (Urbana and Chicago: University of Illinois Press, 1986) plus *The Urban Crucible* and *Forging Freedom: The Formation of Philadelphia's Black Community, 1720–1840* (Cambridge, MA: Harvard University Press, 1988); Jean R. Soderlund, *Quakers and Slavery: A Divided Spirit* (Princeton: Princeton University Press, 1985); Graham Russell Hodges, *Slavery and Freedom in the Rural North: African Americans in Monmouth County, New Jersey, 1665–1865* (Madison, WI.: Madison House, 1996) and *Root and Branch: African Americans in New York and East Jersey, 1613–1863* (Chapel Hill: University of North Carolina Press, 1999); and James Oliver Horton and Lois E. Horton, *In Hope of Liberty: Culture, Community and Protest among Northern Free Blacks, 1700–1860* (New York: Oxford University Press, 1997).

Chapter 5 Slave and Servant Resistance

Bacon's Rebellion (1676) was the one revolt in colonial North American history in which slaves and ex-servants combined to pose a threat to social order. Though crushed, it had a long resonance in terms of class and racial relations in the Chesapeake. The significance of Bacon's Rebellion is brought out in Morgan, *American Slavery, American Freedom* and Breen, 'A Changing Labor Force and Race Relations in Virginia'. A full-length study is Wilcomb E. Washburn, *The Governor and the Rebel: A History of Bacon's Rebellion in Virginia* (Chapel Hill: University of North Carolina Press, 1957). The major slave uprising in eighteenth-century North America was the Stono Rebellion in South Carolina in 1739. This revolt has been analyzed in Wood, *Black Majority*; Darold D. Wax, '"The Great Risque We Run": The Aftermath of Slave Rebellion at Stono, South Carolina, 1739–1745', *Journal of Negro History*, 77 (1982), pp. 136–47; John K. Thornton, 'African Dimensions of the Stono Rebellion', *AHR*, 96 (1991), pp. 1101–13; and Edward A. Pearson, '"A Countryside Full of Flames": A Reconsideration of the Stono Rebellion and Slave Rebelliousness in the Early Eighteenth-Century South Carolina Lowcountry', *Slavery and Abolition*, 17 (1996), pp. 22–50. A well-documented attempted slave plot in New York City (1741) is the subject of Thomas J. Davis, *A Rumour of Revolt: the 'Great Negro Plot' in Colonial New York* (New York: Free Press, 1985) and Peter Linebaugh and Marcus Rediker, '"The Outcasts of the Nations of the Earth": The New York Conspiracy of 1741 in Atlantic Perspective' in their *The Many-Headed Hydra: The Adventures of the Atlantic Proletariat* (Boston: Beacon Press, 2000). Three good studies of Gabriel's Conspiracy (1800) have appeared in recent years: Mullin, *Flight and Rebellion*, ch. 5; Douglas R. Egerton, *Gabriel's Rebellion: The Virginia Slave Conspiracies of 1800 and 1802* (Chapel Hill: University of North Carolina Press, 1993) and James Sidbury, *Ploughshares into Swords: Race, Rebellion, and Identity in Gabriel's Virginia, 1730–1810* (New York: Cambridge University Press, 1997).

   A number of studies have explored slave resistance, with particular emphasis on slave mobility and running away. A concise general statement can be found in Peter H. Wood, 'Slave Resistance' in Jacob E. Cooke (ed.), *Encyclopedia of the North American Colonies*, vol. 2 (1993). See also Mullin, *Flight and Rebellion*; Michael Mullin, *Africa in America: Slave Acculturation and Resistance in the American South and British Caribbean, 1736–1831* (Urbana-Champaign, IL: University of Illinois Press, 1992); Marvin L. Michael Kay and Lorin Lee Cary, 'Slave Runaways in Colonial North Carolina, 1748–1775', *North Carolina Historical Review*, 63 (1986), pp. 1–39; Alan D. Watson, 'Impulse towards Independence: Resistance and Rebellion among North Carolina Slaves,

1750–1775,' *Journal of Negro History*, 63 (1978), pp. 317–28; Peter H. Wood, '"Liberty is Sweet": African-American Freedom Struggles in the years before White Independence' in Alfred F. Young (ed.), *Beyond the American Revolution: Explorations in the History of American Radicalism* (De Kalb, IL: University of Northern Illinois Press, 1993), pp. 149–84; Billy G. Smith, 'Runaway Slaves in the Mid-Atlantic Region during the Revolutionary Era' in Ronald Hoffman and Peter J. Albert (eds), *The Transforming Hand of Revolution: Reconsidering the American Revolution as a Social Movement* (Charlottesville, VA: University Press of Virginia, 1996), pp. 199–230; Shane White, 'Black Fugitives in Colonial South Carolina', *Australasian Journal of American Studies*, 1 (1980), pp. 25–40; and Philip D. Morgan, 'Colonial South Carolina Runaways: Their Significance for Slave Culture' in Gad Heuman (ed.), *Out of the House of Bondage: Runaways, Resistance and Marronage in Africa and the New World* (London: Frank Cass, 1986). A particularly useful study is Sylvia R. Frey, *Water from the Rock: Black Resistance in a Revolutionary Age* (Princeton: Princeton University Press, 1991).

Less attention has focused on servant and convict resistance, but overviews of runaways among these groups can be found in Salinger, *'To Serve Well and Faithfully'*, ch. 4; Ekirch, *Bound for America*; and Kenneth Morgan, 'Convict Runaways in Maryland', *Journal of American Studies*, 23 (1989), pp. 253–68. Broader treatments of slave and servant resistance can be found in Rediker, 'Good Hands, Stout Heart, and Fast Feet'; Peter Linebaugh and Marcus Rediker, 'The Many-Headed Hydra: Sailors, Slaves, and the Atlantic Working Class in the Eighteenth Century', *Journal of Historical Sociology*, 3 (1990), pp. 225–52; and Jonathan Prude, 'To Look Upon the "Lower Sort": Runaway Ads and the Appearance of Unfree Laborers in America, 1750–1800', *JAH*, 78 (1991), pp. 124–60. Collections of advertisements for fugitive slaves include Lathan A. Windley's *Runaway Slave Advertisements: A Documentary History from the 1730s to 1790*, 4 vols (Westport, CT: Greenwood Press, 1983); Billy G. Smith and Richard Wojtowicz (eds), *Blacks who Stole Themselves: Advertisements for Runaways in the Pennsylvania Gazette, 1728–1790* (Philadelphia, PA: University of Pennsylvania Press, 1989); and Graham Russell Hodges and Alan Edward Brown, *'Pretends to be Free': Runaway Slave Advertisements from Colonial and Revolutionary New York and New Jersey* (New York: Garland, 1994).

Chapter 6 Slavery and Freedom in the Revolutionary Era

Helpful introductions to the major themes connected with slavery, race and abolitionism in the revolutionary era include Kolchin, *American Slavery*, ch. 3; Duncan J. MacLeod, *Slavery, Race and the American Revolution* (Cambridge: Cambridge University Press, 1974); Sylvia R. Frey, 'Liberty, Equality, and Slavery: The Paradox of the American Revolution' in Jack P. Greene (ed.), *The American Revolution: Its Character and Limits* (New York: New York University Press, 1987); and Gary B. Nash, *Race and Revolution* (Madison, WI: Madison House, 1990). Nash's text includes a useful selection of relevant primary documents. A classic statement of the inextricable links between slavery and liberty in an age when American statesmen espoused natural rights' theory is Edmund S. Morgan's 'Slavery and Freedom: The American Paradox', *JAH*, 59 (1972), pp. 5–29, reprinted in his book *The Challenge of the American Revolution* (New York: W. W. Norton, 1976). These works include material on the growth of anti-slavery ideas and the spread of notions of gradual abolition. Much more on these issues can be found in Rice, *The Rise and Fall of Black Slavery*; Jordan, *White over Black*; and David Brion Davis, *The Problem of Slavery in the Age of Revolution, 1770–1823* (Ithaca, NY: Cornell University Press, 1975), a magisterial work. Jean Soderlund's *Quakers and Slavery: A Divided Spirit* (Princeton: Princeton University Press, 1985) demonstrates how even the Religious Society of Friends, a group at the forefront of abolitionist activity, nevertheless took decades to condemn slave trading and slaveholding. For pro-slavery arguments, see Fredrika Teute Schmidt and Barbara Ripel Wilhelm, 'Early Proslavery Petitions in Virginia', *WMQ*, 70 (1973), pp. 133–46, and Larry E. Tise, *Proslavery: A History of the Defense of Slavery in America, 1701–1840* (Athens, GA: University of Georgia Press, 1988).

The ambiguous relationship between slavery and the Declaration of Independence is covered in Jack P. Greene, 'All Men are Created Equal: Some Reflections on the Character of the American Revolution' in his *Imperatives, Behaviors, and Identities: Essays in Early American Cultural History* (Charlottesville, VA: University Press of Virginia, 1992), ch. 10. Studies of the position of blacks during the War of Independence include Benjamin Quarles, *The Negro in the American Revolution* (Chapel Hill: University of North Carolina Press, 1961) and Philip S. Foner, *Blacks in the American Revolution* (Westport, CT: Greenwood Press, 1976). A more nuanced account has appeared recently in Frey's

Water from the Rock, a book that can also be read as a narrative of the course of the War of Independence in the southern states.

Studies of the Founding Fathers' attitudes towards slavery can be found in several books already cited, notably Jordan's *White over Black* and Davis's *The Problem of Slavery in the Age of Revolution*. For an interesting insight into the changing interpretation of the topic by one historian, compare William W. Freehling, 'The Founding Fathers and Slavery', *AHR*, 77 (1972), pp. 81–93, anthologized in Allen Weinstein and Frank Otto Gatell (ed.), *American Negro Slavery: A Modern Reader*, 2nd edn (New York: Oxford University Press, 1973), pp. 207–23, with the same author's 'The Founding Fathers, Conditional Antislavery, and the Nonradicalism of the American Revolution' in *The Reintegration of American History: Slavery and the Civil War* (New York: Oxford University Press, 1994). Most attention on the Founding Fathers' approach to slavery has focused on Jefferson, though there are useful studies of Washington and Madison too. Dissection of Jefferson's seemingly contradictory stance on race and slavery has been more critical of late. A reading of the following studies will confirm this: William Cohen, 'Thomas Jefferson and the Problem of Slavery', *JAH*, 56 (1969), pp. 503–26; Merrill D. Peterson, *Thomas Jefferson and the New Nation: A Biography* (New York: Oxford University Press, 1970); Paul Finkelman, 'Jefferson and Slavery: "Treason against the hopes of the World"' in Peter S. Onuf (ed.), *Jeffersonian Legacies* (Charlottesville, VA: University Press of Virginia, 1993), pp. 181–221; Michael Zuckerman, *Almost Chosen People: Oblique Biographies in the American Grain* (Berkeley and Los Angeles, CA: University of California Press, 1993), ch. 6; and Joseph J. Ellis, *American Sphinx: The Character of Thomas Jefferson* (New York: Alfred A. Knopf, 1997). Onuf's volume includes several other significant essays on Jefferson, including Lucia C. Stanton's '"Those Who Labor for my Happiness": Thomas Jefferson and his Slaves', pp. 147–80. The most recent relevant book on Jefferson is Jan Ellen Lewis and Peter S. Onuf (eds), *Sally Hemings and Thomas Jefferson: History, Memory, and Civic Culture* (Charlottesville, VA: University Press of Virginia, 1999). Helpful treatments of Washington and Madison's positions on slavery can be found in Fritz Hirschfeld, *George Washington and Slavery: A Documentary Reader* (Columbia: University of Missouri Press, 1997); Kenneth Morgan, 'George Washington and the Problem of Slavery', *Journal of American Studies*, 34 (2000), Ralph L. Ketcham, *James Madison: A Biography* (New York: Macmillan,

1971); and Drew R. McCoy, 'Slavery' in Robert A. Rutland (ed.), *James Madison and the American Nation 1751–1836: An Encyclopedia* (New York: Simon and Schuster, 1994), pp. 378–80.

How politicians handled the issue of slavery or free soil in the Old North West and the constitutional status of slaves has generated several illuminating studies. On the Northwest Ordinance see, in particular, Paul Finkelman, 'Slavery and the Northwest Ordinance: A Study in Ambiguity', *Journal of the Early Republic*, 6 (1986), pp. 343–70; Peter S. Onuf, *Statehood and Union: A History of the Northwest Ordinance* (Bloomington, IN: Indiana University Press, 1987); and David Brion Davis, 'The Significance of Excluding Slavery from the Old Northwest in 1787', *Indiana Magazine of History*, 84 (1988), pp. 75–89. Finkelman is critical of the lack of commitment to anti-slavery displayed by the committee that framed the Ordinance, while Davis stresses its accomplishment in prohibiting the extension of slavery to a significant westward land mass within the United States. Staughton Lynd, 'The Compromise of 1787', *Political Science Quarterly*, 81 (1966), pp. 225–50, draws illuminating parallels between the handling of slavery in the Northwest Ordinance and in the US Constitution. On the debates over slavery in Philadelphia in the summer of 1787, see, among many studies, Paul Finkelman, 'Slavery and the Constitutional Convention: Making a Covenant with Death' in Richard R. Beeman, Stephen Botein and Edward C. Carter II (eds), *Beyond Confederation: Origins of the Constitution and American National Identity* (Chapel Hill: University of North Carolina Press, 1987), pp. 188–225; and William M. Wiecek, 'The Witch at the Christening: Slavery and the Constitution's Origins' in Leonard W. Levy and Dennis J. Mahoney (eds), *The Framing and Ratification of the Constitution* (London: Macmillan, 1987). The two essays by Finkelman and Lynd's important article are reprinted in Paul Finkelman (ed.), *Articles on American Slavery: vol. 4: Slavery, Revolutionary America, and the New Nation* (New York: Garland Publishing, Inc., 1989). Useful context on the political handling of the slavery issue is contained in Donald L. Robinson, *Slavery in the Structure of America Politics 1765–1820* (New York: Harcourt Brace Jovanovich, 1971). For the centrality of slavery to constitutional debates in the Palmetto state, see Robert M. Weir, 'South Carolina: Slavery and the Structure of the Union' in Michael Allen Gillespie and Michael Lienesch (eds), *Ratifying the Constitution* (Lawrence, KS: University of Kansas Press, 1989), pp. 201–34. A splendid collection of contemporary commentary on slavery, race and the American government can be found in John P. Kaminski (ed.), *A Necessary Evil? Slavery and the Debate over the Constitution* (Madison, WI: Madison House, 1995).

The changing regional context of race, slavery and manumission in the revolutionary era received close attention in Ira Berlin and Ronald Hoffman (eds), *Slavery and Freedom in the Age of the American Revolution* (Charlottesville, VA: University Press of Virginia, 1986). The contributions by Gary B. Nash, Richard S. Dunn and Philip D. Morgan – on, respectively, the emancipation experience in the northern seaport cities, black society in the Chesapeake and black society in the Low-country – are especially insightful. Berlin has contributed several other notable studies to black life in late eighteenth-century America: *Slaves without Masters: The Free Negro in the Antebellum South* (New York: Pantheon Books, 1974); 'The Revolution in Black Life' in Alfred F. Young (ed.), *The American Revolution: Explorations in American Radicalism* (De Kalb, IL: Northern Illinois University Press, 1976), pp. 349–82; and *Many Thousands Gone*. Some of the best writing on slavery and freedom in the period of the American Revolution can be found in regional studies such as Morgan, *Slave Counterpoint*; Russell R. Menard, 'Slavery, Economic Growth, and Revolutionary Ideology in the South Carolina Lowcountry' in Ronald Hoffman, John J. McCusker, Russell R. Menard and Peter J. Albert (eds), *The Economy of Early America: The Revolutionary Period, 1763–1790* (Charlottesville, VA: University Press of Virginia, 1987), pp. 244–74; Hodges, *Slavery and Freedom in the Rural North*; Nash, *Forging Freedom*; Shane White, *Somewhat More Independent: The End of Slavery in New York City, 1770–1810* (Athens, GA: University of Georgia Press, 1991); Gary B. Nash and Jean R. Soderlund, *Freedom by Degrees: Emancipation in Pennsylvania and its Aftermath* (New York: Oxford University Press, 1991); and T. H. Breen, 'Making History: The Force of Public Opinion and the Last Years of Slavery in Revolutionary Massachusetts' in Ronald Hoffman, Mechal Sobel, and Fredrika J. Teute (eds), *Through a Glass Darkly: Reflections on Personal Identity in Early America* (Chapel Hill: University of North Carolina Press, 1997), pp. 67–95. For a still useful overview of northern abolitionism, see Arthur Zilversmit, *The First Emancipation: The Abolition of Slavery in the North* (Chicago: University of Chicago Press, 1967).

Index